Marriages (1895–1905) and
Deaths (1895–1900)
and Related Items
Abstracted from

THE GOLDEN NEW ERA

of Golden, Adams County, Illinois

Mrs. Joseph J. Beals
& Sandra Kirchner

HERITAGE BOOKS
2021

HERITAGE BOOKS

AN IMPRINT OF HERITAGE BOOKS, INC.

Books, CDs, and more—Worldwide

For our listing of thousands of titles see our website
at
www.HeritageBooks.com

Published 2021 by
HERITAGE BOOKS, INC.
Publishing Division
5810 Ruatan Street
Berwyn Heights, Md. 20740

International Standard Book Number
Paperbound: 978-0-7884-0792-5

Table of Contents

Preface

The death and marriage items in this book were abstracted from *The Golden New Era* newspapers of Golden Illinois. These papers were dated from 1879 through 1900. In the early 1960s, while doing research on my genealogy in *The Golden New Era*, I found so much valuable information that I decided to start writing it down on index cards. Items that mentioned a family name would be written on a 3 x 5 index card. Cards for any advertising, jury lists, criminal courts, and letters left at the post office were also made. Remaining items will be worked up for publishing as time permits.

AARON, Miss Anna   Apr 18, 1901
    See McCune, John
AARON, Miss Edna   York Neck   Jan 8, 1898
    Wedding at Mr and Mrs Cale Aaron's last Wednesday--Mr Lawless of Columbus
    and Miss Edna Aaron of Big Neck, were the contracting parties.
AARON, Miss Edna V.   Jan 1, 1898
    See Lawless, Wm B.
AARON, Dr H.   Big Neck   Aug 26, 1904
    Dr H. Aaron and wife of Oklahoma are here on their wedding tour. His sis-
    ter, Mrs Anna McCune, of Oklahoma, is also home on a visit.
AARON, Miss Hetty   Oct 2, 1903
    See Miller, Charles
ACKLAM, Charles and May   Local   Jun 6, 1896
    Charles Acklam commenced suit for divorce yesterday from May Acklam says
    they were married Camp Point Friday 17, 1890 and live together until the
    following March 1, 11 days. He charged her with infidelity in 1895.
ACKLAM, Chas. and Mary   Miserable Married Men   Jul 4, 1896
    Divorce decree signed--Chas. Acklam vs Mary Acklam. She is now living
    somewhere in Hancock County.
ACKLEM, Miss Jennie E.   January 1893   Jan 17, 1901
    See Hirons, Wm
ACKLEM, Miss Mary   February 1893   Feb 21, 1901
    See Felsman, Albert
ADAIR, Curtis   Local   Oct 2, 1903
    Curtis Adair, formerly of Keene township, and Miss Eva A. Follum, of
    Hulls, were married this week.
ADAIR, Henry and Sarah   Local   Sep 14, 1899
    In the Quincy Whig of last week appeared the mention of a divorce suit in
    which Henry L. Adair had asked for a divorce from his wife, Sarah Adair.
    Henry L. of Clayton read the notice and almost dropped dead from surprise.
    He hurried to Quincy and found the couple were from Quincy and had the
    same names as he and his wife.
ADAIR, Rev J.R.   York Neck   Oct 12, 1899
    Rev J.R. Adair took himself a new bride Wednesday, a young widow of 70
    summers. She lived near Marcelline.
ADAMS, Miss Hattie B.   5 Years Ago   Feb 13, 1897
    Miss Hattie B. Adams was married to John B. Gerjets by Rev Oet.
ADAMS, Isaac   Camp Point   Dec 22, 1898
    Isaac Adams and Miss Mollie Hudson were married last Thursday eve and will
    go to housekeeping on the Ben Earl property.
ADAMS, Luenia   Dec 25, 1897
    See McCune, Hughey
ADAMS, Prof W.T.   Married   May 15, 1897
    Thursday occurred the marriage of Prof. W.T. Adams and Miss Emma Smith.
    They drove to Camp Point in the AM and took the fast mail for Quincy
    where they were married by Rev Dana. Miss Smith is daughter of Daniel
    Smith of this city.
ADEN, George   Married   Feb 22, 1896
    Married last Thursday eve two of North Easts' popular german people,
    George Aden of Chatten and Miss Mamie Buss, daughter of Mr and Mrs R.A.
    Buss who live near the railroad about a mile and half from town, by
    Rev Darrow of the East Side German Church. Will live on Mr Buss's farm
    near Elm Grove,
ADEN, Jasper   Feb 27, 1902
    See Schone, Minnie

ADEN, Ranke H.   Local   Feb 8, 1896
    Marriage license issued to Ranke H. Aden and Miss Christina Shone, both
    of Golden.
AGNEW, Walter   Augusta   Jun 26, 1897
    Walter Agnew and bride, of Quincy are guests of relatives.
AKERS, Mr Ira   Wedding   Nov 8, 1900
    Married, Mr Ira Akers, of LaPrairie and Miss Alice Lee of Bowen at the
    home of Elder and Mrs Harry G. Vandervoort on the eve of October 17th.
    Wedding party included Misses Jennie Lee and Pearl Akers, sisters of
    bride and groom. Will live Golden where Mr Akers is in railway station.
AKERS, Miss Pearl   California Wedding   Sep 9, 1904
    Miss Pearl Akers, eldest daughter of Mr and Mrs A.J. Akers and Mr Leslie
    Walter Raley were married, Thursday Aug 18, 1904, 8 PM at the Advent
    Christian Church, Lordsburg, Cal. by Rev W.O. Tingle. Relatives and few
    friends were invited to the home of brides parents for refreshments.
    Groom has been a resident of Lordsburg for past two years having immi-
    grated from Texas. His occupation is photographer and he is also a
    farmer. Will live Lordsburg.
AKERS, Mr Posey   Elm Grove   Apr 18, 1901
    Mr Posey Akers and Miss Lizzie McLeod, of Tazewell County Virginia arrived
    from there on an elopement and were married at Hotel Golden in Golden
    last Thursday. There seems to have been no valid reason for the objections
    of parents nor any great necessity for an elopement, as the parties are of
    legal age to elect for themselves to marry without restriction. They will
    work for J.H. Balfour.
ALBERS, Miss Jennie   Feb 23, 1899
    See Techt, William M.
ALESHIRE, Wm   Local   Nov 21, 1902
    Wm Aleshire and Miss May McWhorter, of Plymouth were married at Quincy
    last week.
ALEXANDER, Miss Eva   Elm Grove   Sep 1, 1898
    Miss Eva Alexander and Homer Champion will be married Wednesday if all
    reports are true at residence of Geo. Eastman near Augusta.
ALEXANDER, Miss Eva   Sep 1, 1898
    See Champion, Homer
ALEXANDER, Fredonia B.   Wedding Bells   May 15, 1902
    About 70 guests assembled at the residence of J.T. Alexander on Thursday
    afternoon, May 8, 1902 to witness the marriage of their daughter, Fredonia
    B. to Wm Martin McGinnis at 3 PM. Miss Leota Aull took her place at
    organ and played the bridal chorus. Bridesmaids were, Miss Alta Severns
    and Miss Hila Hackney. Rites conducted by Rev C.H. Gordon, pastor of
    U.B. Church. Groom is prosperous farmer. Reception held next day at
    home of groom.
ALEXANDER, Mr O.W.   Jul 26, 1900
    See Burke, Miss Jessie
ALEXANDER, P.L.   Married   Oct 31, 1902
    Married and not reported, last week, P.L. Alexander and Miss Grace Robbins
    at the home of brides parents in Quincy on Oct. 9. P.L. Alexander of
    Redfield, S.D. and Miss Grace Robbins were married at high noon yesterday
    at the home of parents of bride, Mr and Mrs Jas. H. Robbins, 1229 Ken-
    tucky St by Rev R.E. Mathis of Payson. Reception will be today at home
    of parents of the groom near Elm Grove. Groom is a practicing attorney
    at Redfield, S.D. and son of Daniel Alexander, one of the oldest residents
    of North East township. Went to Redfield about a year ago. Will live
    Redfield.   "Quincy Whig"

ALEXANDER, Miss Pearl   Oct 20, 1898
    See Underwood, George
ALEXANDER, Sid   Local   Feb 15, 1902
    Sid Alexander will return today from Virginia with his bride, who was
    formerly Miss Ada Hagy.
ALEXANDER, Sidney W.   Elm Grove   Feb 13, 1902
    Invitations are out for a dinner reception at the home of Mr and Mrs
    Daniel Alexander for next Thursday, in honor of their son, Sidney W.
    Alexander, and bride, who is a Virginia lady. In the evening the young
    folks are also invited for a social.
ALEXANDER, William   Pine Grove   Sep 1, 1898
    William Alexander of this place and Miss Carrie Walker of Elm Grove were
    married last Tuesday.
ALEXANDER, Wm   Local   Sep 1, 1898
    Wm Alexander and Miss Carrie Walker were married at Quincy Tuesday. Both
    are well known in the Elm Grove district.
ALEXANDER, Wm   Elm Grove   Sep 1, 1898
    Wm Alexander and Miss Carrie Walker were married last Tuesday eve at home
    of brides father, C.W. Walker.
ALLEN, Cora M.   Oct 9, 1897
    See Edmunds, James
ALLEN, Miss Gertrude   Jan 29, 1904
    See Grose, Henry K.
ALLEN, Miss Lulu   Jan 22, 1898
    See Hornecker, Edwin
ANDERSON, Mr and Mrs H.S.   Clayton   Nov 24, 1898
    Mr and Mrs H.S. Anderson returned from Missouri Thursday night and on Fri-
    day Mr and Mrs C.S. Anderson served an infair dinner to the bride and
    groom. The young married couple will live with brides mother.
ANDERSON, Herma L.   Married at Quincy   Jun 24, 1904
    Herma L. Anderson and Miss Carrie Hightower, both of Huntsville were mar-
    ried in the office of County Clerk Pearce Wednesday afternoon by Rev.
    Parker Shields. Mr and Mrs Clem L. Hawkins, of Golden, uncle and aunt
    of the bride were present.   "Whig"
ANDERSON, Miss Jennie Amoret   Wedding   Aug 12, 1904
    Last evening at the home of brides parents, two miles north of LaPrairie,
    occurred the wedding of Miss Jennie Amoret Anderson to Mr Roy Taylor Beckett
    by Rev D.H. Hartley. This AM the couple will come to Golden where they
    will be tendered arreception at the home of grooms parents Mr and Mrs
    George Beckett. They will live on a farm belonging to grooms father,
    situated two miles north of Camp Point.
ANDREWS, Miss Cella   Oct 17, 1896
    See Witt, William
ARBOGAST, Clayton   Local   Jan 29, 1904
    Mrs Chris Detmers and children and Mrs Ella Franzen attended wedding of
    Clayton Arbogast and Miss Mary Franzen at Bentley Wednesday.
ARGAST, Will   Local   Sep 22, 1898
    Our friend, Will Argast of the Nauvoo Rustler has decided to desert bach-
    elorhood and we have received invitation to attend wedding at Madison,
    Wisconsin October 5th. The lady is Miss Katherine Hoeveler. She has
    been attending St Marys academy at Nauvoo.
ARNOLD, Otho M.   Local   Oct 27, 1905
    Otho N. Arnold, formerly of Big Neck, now a clerk in the Quincy postoffice
    married Miss Cora M. Thompson, of Mendon, in Quincy Sunday. Groom is son
    of John Arnold, of Houston.

ARTZ, Miss Gertrude   Oct 25, 1900
  See Scearce, Emmett
ASBURY, Henry and Addie   Miserable Married Men   Jul 4, 1896
  In divorce court, Henry Asbury vs Addie Asbury. Asbury lives in Loraine
  where he was married on St Valentines Day 1891 wife deserted him in Sep-
  tember of same year.
ASHER, Miss Nora   Jan 18, 1900
  See Shake, Marvin A.
ASHER, Warren   York Neck   Dec 30, 1904
  Married Wednesday, Mr Warren Asher and Mrs D.E. Geibert. Will be at home
  to their friends at the Geibert mansion in York Neck.
AULL, Miss E. Blanche   Locals   Mar 24, 1905
  Miss E. Blanche Aull, daughter of Mr and Mrs Joseph E. Aull of Camp Point
  township, was married in Chicago on the 5th inst, to Mr Leo Seligsohn of
  that city.
AUSMUS, Miss   Mar 21, 1901
  See Holecamp, Francis
AUSMUS, Mrs Lulu B.   Dec 23, 1904
  See Watson. Elmer A.
AVERY, Cliff   Augusta   Jul 5, 1900
  Word has been received here of the marriage of Cliff Avery, formerly of
  Augusta but now of Oklahoma.
BACHMAN,   Local   Feb 27, 1897
  Miss Maggie Eilts attended the Bachman-Jurgens wedding in Hancock county
  Tuesday.
BACHMAN, Wm   Feb 27, 1897
  See Jurgens, Miss Lizzie
BACON, R.H. and wife   Golden Wedding   Sep 11, 1897
  R.H. Bacon and wife, of LaPrairie, last Thursday, September 2nd celebrated
  their 50th wedding anniversary.
BACON, Wm Jr.   Local   Dec 21, 1899
  Wm Bacon Jr and Miss Lula Groves, both of Huntsville, were married in
  Quincy on the 14th inst.
BAGBY, C. Edgar   Mar 13, 1902
  See Robbins, Miss Blanche
BAGBY, Chas. Edgar   Mar 13, 1902
  See Robbins, Miss Myrtle Blanche
BAILEY, Thomas   A Quiet Wedding   Apr 18, 1896
  On Monday afternoon at the home of Col and Mrs Hanna, occurred the mar-
  riage of Esquire Thomas Bailey and Mrs P.J. Rhea, both of Camp Point by
  Justice Hanna. Both are known to all the old residents of Adams County.
  Bride is a sister of Mrs Hanna.
BAIRD, Miss Bertha   Sep 8, 1899
  See Wishart. Charlie
BAIRD, Miss Nellie   Local   Jul 29, 1904
  Miss Nellie Baird and Frank Behan, both from Camp Point, were married at
  Galesburg Saturday July 16th.
BAKER, Miss Josie   Dec 23, 1904
  See Stuhrenberg, Henry
BALDWIN, John   Elm Grove   Jun 20, 1901
  Oscar Baldwin with Mr Boman's family, of North Elm Grove, attended the
  wedding of his brother, John Baldwin to Miss Hodgson, both of Clayton,
  last Sunday in the Presbyterian Church.

BALDWIN, O. Darwin   Married   Apr 3, 1903
   At the home of brides parents, Mr and Mrs P.N. Bowman, of near Pine Grove,
   in midst of about 42 guests, O. Darwin Baldwin, of Clayton and Miss Lola
   R. Bowman were married on March 26th by Rev G.L. Bowman, an uncle of the
   bride. Miss Grace Baldwin, sister of the groom, played the wedding march.
   Reception given at home of grooms parents of Clayton, the following day.
   Will live on the Joseph Coffman place near Pine Grove.
BALDWIN, Oscar   Mar 27, 1903
   Oscar Baldwin and Miss Lola Boman, of Elm Grove were married Thursday eve
   by Rev Evans at the home of the brides parents.
BALFOUR, Letha Viola   Aug 7, 1903
   See Hughes, Horace Eben
BALL, James   Mar 28, 1896
   See Davis, Mrs Nancy
BARGER, D. Austin   Bowen   Nov 23, 1895
   Married Thursday November 14th D. Austin Barger and Miss Lennie Wade at the
   home of brides parents, Mr and Mrs Wade of Plymouth, Ill.
BARKER, George   Mar 28, 1896
   See Sawtelle, Miss Lillie
BARLEY, Miss Carrie   Augusta   Oct 4, 1900
   Mrs Will Newland left last week for Waynesville, Ohio, where she will
   attend the wedding of her sister, Miss Carrie Barley.
BARNES, Miss Pearl   Dec 20, 1900
   See Shroat, Bartlett
BARTELLS, Bartell   Local   Mar 14, 1896
   Bartell Bartells and Miss Depka Saathoff were married at the East German
   Church Friday eve, March 6th by Rev Darrow.
BARTELLS, Miss Lottie   Sep 25, 1897
   See Sheley, Walter
BARTELLS, Miss Rosa   May 30, 1901
   See Cummings, Tom
BARTELLS, Miss Rosa   Camp Point   May 30, 1901
   Mrs Anna Oblander and children, of Bushnell, came down to attend the wed-
   ding of her sister, Miss Rosa Bartells.
BATES, Dr Lee   Camp Point   Sep 21, 1899
   On Thursday eve of last week at the home of Dr and Mrs S. Henry occurred
   the marriage of their youngest daughter, Fannie to Dr Lee Bates. Ceremony
   was performed on the lawn by Rev T.M. Dillen.
BATES, Dr Lee   Camp Point   Sep 21, 1899
   Mrs May Anderson of Martinsburg, Iowa and Mrs Anna McFarland of Atlantic,
   Iowa and Drs Walter and Ed Henry of Omaha were here to attend the wedding
   of their sister, Miss Fannie, to Dr Lee Bates.
BATES, Will   Camp Point   Oct 5, 1899
   The wedding of Will Bates to Miss Lillie Mensedike will take place at the
   home of the bride on Thursday eve of this week.
BAUER, William   Henry, NE   Feb 6, 1902
   Married recently, William Bauer and Miss Etta Folkers.
BEAL, Miss Irene   Augusta   Mar 8, 1900
   H.P. Bredette, our C.B. & Q. agent, to Miss Irene Beal, of Macomb, were
   married at the home of the brides sister, Mrs F.G. McClellan, by Rev Jos
   Sanderson, of this place. They came down from Augusta on the evening
   train and are living in Mr Bredette's home on East Green St. He has been
   our agent here for about 25 years and was born and raised here. Bride is
   sister of Mrs E.C. Maguire

BEAL, Mrs Lena   Oct 20, 1898
  See Ward, Walter S.
BEARD, Ina Pearl   Feb 7, 1901
  See McGinnis, Clyde
BECKETT, Miss Bessie   Wedding   Jun 24, 1904
  On Wednesday at 5 PM at the home of brides parents, Mr and Mrs Geo. R.
  Beckett, occurred the wedding of Miss Bessie, to Mr Edward Wilson Fuhr
  by D.H. Hartley. Mr Fuhr's home is in Macomb, is an operator in the
  service of the CB & Q.
BECKETT, Clarence   Camp Point   Feb 9, 1899
  Invitations are out for wedding of Clarence Beckett and Miss Lizzie
  McFarland February 15th at 6 o'clock.
BECKETT, Clarence E.   Local   Feb 9, 1899
  Invitations are out for marriage of Miss Lizzie McFarland and Clarence E.
  Beckett. Mrs McFarland is daughter of Albert McFarland who lives mid-
  way between Camp Point and Golden.
BECKETT, Clarence E.   Married   Feb 23, 1899
  Quiet wedding that united the lives of Clarence E. Beckett, of Shelbina,
  Missouri and Miss Lizzie O. McFarland, of Camp Point at the paternal home
  of Mr and Mrs A.H. McFarland, Wednesday at 6:30 PM February 15th.
  Swedish wedding march was played while bride and groom entered the parlor
  unattended. Ceremony by Rev T.M. Dillion of Camp Point. Groom is son of
  W.T. Beckett of Camp Point and is a graduate of Camp Point High School
  in class of "95". He is a prosperous farmer of Shelbina.
BECKETT, Miss Cora   May 31. 1900
  See Dickhut, Clarence
BECKETT, Miss Della   Nov 18, 1893   Jan 30, 1902
  See Stinson, C.W.
BECKETT, Miss Ella   Dec 5, 1901
  See Brierton, James F.
BECKETT, Fred   Local   May 31, 1900
  Cards of invitation has been received in Golden announcing the wedding of
  Fred Beckett and Miss Ola Parsons, of Garden City, Kansas on June 6th.
  Will live Independence, Kansas after July 6th.
BECKETT, Mrs H.I.   Local   Nov 16, 1895
  George Carlin and family attended wedding anniversary of Mr and Mrs H.I.
  Beckett and visited friends in Golden this week.
BECKETT, Harry I.   Local   Nov 16, 1895
  Monday was the 3rd anniversary of Harry I. Beckett and wife and friends
  were invited to partake of turkey, etc.
BECKETT, Harry I.   5 Years Ago   Nov 13, 1897
  Harry I. Beckett and Miss Dora Duis were married.
BECKETT, Miss Ida   Local   Nov 6, 1897
  Miss Ida Beckett attended wedding of a cousin near Bowen Wednesday.
BECKETT, Jno.   Mar 7, 1896
  See Selby, Miss Ellect B.
BECKETT, John   Camp Point   Mar 14, 1896
  John Beckett and Miss Electa Selby of Golden were married by Rev Dilley,
  at his home, last Wednesday.
BECKETT, Mr and Mrs John   Local   Mar 31, 1905
  Mr and Mrs John Beckett invited relatives and friends in to help celebrate
  their 10th wedding anniversary.
BECKETT, Mr and Mrs Joseph A.   Local   Jan 27, 1905
  Children and grandchildren of Mr and Mrs Joseph A. Beckett planned a
  surprise on their parents in the way of a celebration of the 38th anniversary of their marriage last Tuesday. Supper was served.

BECKETT, Miss Laura E.   Feb 26, 1904
   See Marshall, Charles H.
BECKETT, Miss Lottie   Jun 5, 1903
   See Ward, John Omer
BECKETT, Mr R.M.   Jan 17, 1901
   See Carlin, Miss Hattie B.
BECKETT, Roy Taylor   Aug 12, 1904
   See Anderson, Miss Jennie Amoret
BEER, Miss Bertha E.   Sep 4, 1903
   See Kinchloe, H.E.
BEER, C.E.   Jan 24, 1901
   See Herring, Miss Edith
BEER, Irwin   Local   Oct 9, 1903
   Irwin Beer and Miss Alice Frederick, of this village were married at the
   home of brides parents, in west part of town Wednesday eve by Rev Hartley.
   Will live in Golden.
BEER, John and wife   York Neck   Oct 12, 1899
   A grand reception last Monday eve at home of Mr and Mrs Thomas Beer in
   honor of their son John and his newly wedded wife.
BEHAN, Frank   Jul 29, 1904
   See Baird, Miss Nellie
BEHRENS, Miss Frederika   Jul 26, 1900
   See Gerjets, John D.
BEHRENS, Miss Lena   Nov 20, 1903
   See Saathoff, Frank
BEHRENS, Miss Rika   Apr 24, 1897
   See Totsch, Albert
BEHRENS, Ulfert   German Center   Apr 10, 1897
   A marriage license has been issued to Ulfert Behrens and Anna Lubben.
BEHRENS, Ulfert Jr.   Local   Oct 2, 1896
   By the Quincy papers we learn that a marriage license has been issued to
   Ulfert Behrens Jr and Miss Grace Mentz, of this place.
BEHRENS, Weert   Local   Dec 2, 1904
   Our friends Weert Behrens and Freda Buhr hied themselves to Quincy on
   Thursday of last week and returned Mr and Mrs Behrens. The young couple
   have moved to a farm southeast of Golden.
BEINHOFF, Harm   Locals   Feb 24, 1905
   Mr Harm Beinhoff and Miss Lena Stubbins were married at Trinity Church,
   in Golden, at 3 PM Wednesday by Rev H. Dorrow. Reception was held at the
   brides home Wednesday eve. Will live on the property Mr Beinhoff pur-
   chased from Ed Willard.
BELL, John   Pea Ridge   Feb 22, 1896
   John Bell and Miss Mary House of Clayton were married Wednesday eve of
   last week at Clayton.
BELL, John   Pea Ridge   Mar 14, 1896
   John Bell who was lately married will shortly move to the house now oc-
   cupied by Joseph Bell.
BENNET, Miss Daisy   Jan 26, 1899
   See Horney, Earl
BENNETT, Alvin   Local   Jul 24, 1902
   Alvin Bennett of Houston township and Mrs Maggie Dawson, of Plymouth, were
   married at the Occidental Hotel in Quincy last Thursday. Mr Bennett is a
   substantial farmer of Houston. Will live at the Bennett home place.
BENNETT, Freddie   Local   Apr 10, 1903
   Freddie Bennett and Miss Osa Suter, of Houston township, were married last
   week. Groom is son of Alvin Bennett and bride is daughter of John Suter.

BENNETT, Tommy   Locals   Mar 6, 1903
    Tommy Bennett, of Houston township and Miss Anna Miller of Camp Point
    township were married this week.
BERINGER, Fred   Local   Jan 15, 1904
    Fred Beringer and Miss Anna Kern were married at Shelbina, Missouri on
    Thursday of last week. Bride is daughter of George Kern and both con-
    tracting parties are well known in this vicinity.
BERRIAN, Miss Mary   Dec 2, 1893   Feb 6, 1892
    See Ballard, Chas. on supplement page.
BERRIER, George   La Prairie   Jul 7, 1905
    George Berrier, of Camp Point, and Miss Odessa Queen, of this village
    were married Wednesday eve of last week at the parsonage by Rev Evans.
BIENHOFF, Henry   Local   Mar 21, 1901
    On Wednesday of last week at the West Side German Lutherna Church, Henry
    Bienhoff and Miss Emma Whitland were married by Rev Alpers.
Bienhoff, John   Local   Mar 15, 1900
    John Bienhoff and Miss Mary Post were married last Friday afternoon in
    West Side German Lutheran Church by Rev Alpers. Will live Bowen.
BLACK, Clarence   Local   Jun 17, 1904
    Clarence Black, who was at one time located in Golden, and Miss Grace
    Agnes Swaney were married at Clayton on Sunday, June 5th.
BLACK, Ethel   Bowen   Dec 18, 1903
    Miss Mabel Dunlap attended the wedding of Ethel Black and Arthur Horney
    at Denver on Wednesday of last week.
BLACK, Mr Irvin   Dec 24, 1896
    See Bottorff, Miss Rosa
BLACK, Ivin   5 Years Ago   Jan 22, 1898
    Ivin Black and Miss Rosa Bottorff were married.
BLACK, Ivin   December 1892   Dec 27, 1900
    December 24--Ivin Black and Miss Rosa Bottorff were married.
BLACK, Mrs Lizzie   Jun 13, 1901
    See Carlin, J.T.
BLACK, Mrs Mary Elizabeth   Jun 13, 1901
    See Carlin, James T.
BLACK, Mr and Mrs Samuel   Married 50 Years   Dec 8, 1905
    Mr and Mrs Samuel Black, of Black Station, celebrated their 50th wedding
    anniversary Monday December 4th. Immedeite relatives and few friends
    were invited to dinner--present were: Mr and Mrs James Bottorff and Mrs
    Tom Cripper, of Clayton, Mr and Mrs W.L. Black of Kansas City, Missouri,
    Miss Carrie Hollock of Chicago, Mr and Mrs J.A. Beckett and daughter,
    Urith, of Golden, Mr and Mrs Ivin Black, Mr and Mrs Chris Hollock and
    Mrs Harriet Garner of the immediate neighborhood and Rev and Mrs Wilbur
    Huffer of Clayton. Uncle Sam is still hale and hearty and promises to
    make good for years to come and Mrs Black still enjoys fair health.
BLANSETT, Miss Cora   Nov 16, 1895
    See Williams, George
BLANSETT, Luther   Pea Ridge   Jul 5, 1900
    Luther Blansett and Mabel Ruby were married at Squire Lamberts Sunday AM.
BLOCK, Hannah   Weyerts, NE   Mar 9, 1899
    Miss Annie Folkerts and her grandfather, John Kahman left for Gothenburg,
    Nebraska last Tuesday to attend the marriage of Anna's cousin, Hannah Block
BLOOD, Charlie   Camp Point   Sep 8, 1899
    Charlie Blood, one of the leading merchants and Miss Grace Rhea, Milliner,
    went to Chicago last week to purchase goods for their store and while there
    were married at the home of Mr and Mrs Frank Allen. Mrs Allen was formerly
    Miss Hattie Blood.

BLOOD, Katherine S.   Jun 8, 1899
    See Dumney, Herbert C.
BOETTCHER, Mrs Mary   Apr 15, 1904
    See Seehusen, John
BOGER, Arthur C.   Local .   Dec 11, 1903
    At Bushnell, Wednesday of last week Arthur C. Boger and Miss Flora May
    Cutter, of Camp Point were married. Both are members of prominent families
    of Camp Point and will make that village their home.
BOGER, J. Fred   Mar 7, 1896
    See Rhea, Miss Effie
BOGER, Lawrence   Camp Point   May 1, 1897
    Lawrence Boger and Miss Gertrude Jewell were married at the home of the
    bride last Wednesday eve by Rev A.N. Simmons.
BOGER, Lon   Apr 24, 1897
    See Jewell, Miss Gertie
BOLING, Miss Elfa   May 6, 1904
    See Marshall. Lorin
BOMAN, Miss Lola   Mar 27, 1903
    See Baldwin, Oscar
BOMAN, Miss Ola   Jan 3, 1901
    See Stark, C.H.
BOTTORFF, Anderson   5 Years Ago   Jan 22, 1898
    Anderson Bottorff and Miss Cora Omer were married in this city.
BOTTORFF, Anderson   January 1893   Jan 3, 1901
    January 7, Anderson Bottorff and Miss Cora Omer were married.
BOTTORFF, Mrs Cora   Local   Oct 23, 1897
    Mrs Cora Bottorff was married to Edward Ogle, at Peoria, Sunday eve at the
    home of Mr and Mrs L.O. Sutton.
BOTTORFF, Harry   Weds at Keokuk   Oct 20, 1905
    Harry Bottorff and Miss Mabel Hodgson went to Keokuk, Iowa Saturday AM,
    where they were married in the afternoon by Justice H.C. Landers. They
    had to go out of state on account of the for,er Mrs Bottorff having
    secured a divorce from Mr Bottorff at a recent term of the Adams County
    Circuit Court, and the law passed by the past legislature forbidding him
    from marrying in the state within a year. Bottorff is a Golden man and
    was recently acquitted in Quincy of burglary, on technicality. Will
    live in St Louis.   Quincy Journal
BOTTORFF, Miss Jennie   8 Years Ago   Dec 12, 1901
    See Hoyt, B.F.
BOTTORFF, Otis   Fairview   May 29, 1902
    Wm Howard and wife and Mrs Mary Owen attended wedding of Otis Bottorff and
    Miss Abbey Thompson last Sunday afternoon at 3 by Squire Rockenfield.
    Left Monday AM for Kewanee, Illinois where they will make their home.
BOTTORFF, Miss Rosa   Local   Dec 24, 1896
    Marriage of Miss Rosa Bottorff of near LaPrairie, to Mr Irvin Black of
    Black's Station occurred at high noon Wednesday at the home of brides
    parents.
BOTTORFF, Miss Rosa   December 1892   Dec 27, 1900
    See Black, Ivin
BOTTORFF, Miss Rose   5 Years Ago   Jan 22, 1898
    See Black, Ivin
BOWER, George H.   Local   Jun 3, 1904
    George H. Bower of Fall Creek, and Miss Carrie Johnson, of LaPrairie,
    were married this week.

BOWER, George H.   LaPrairie   Jun 10, 1904
    Wedding of George H. Bower, of Fall Creek, and Miss Carrie Johnson, of
    LaPrairie occurred on Wednesday of last week at the home of bride's
    sister, Mr Chas. Heinicke.
BOWMAN, Miss Lola R.   Apr 3, 1903
    See Baldwin, O. Darwin.
BOYD, Miss Mary   Mar 5, 1904
    See Thompson, Wm O.
BOYD, Rob   Houston   Jan 3, 1901
    Mrs Orvel Harris attended the wedding of her brother, Rob Boyd, at
    Denver, Illinois, on Christmas Day.
BOYD, Rob   Houston   Jan 3, 1901
    Mrs Orvel Harris attended the wedding of her brother, Rob Boyd, at Denver,
    Illinois, on Christmas Day.
BOYD, Robert   Fairview   Jan 3, 1901
    Mr Robert Boyd, of Fairview, was married to Miss Alta Burnett, of Bentley,
    Christmas Day.
BOYTZ, Miss Myrtle   Dec 22, 1898
    See Robertson, Chas.
BRADLEY, Miss Blanch   Jan 3, 1901
    See Orth, Will
BRADLEY, Wm C.   Sep 8, 1905
    See Franks, Miss Nonae
BRADNEY, Miss Belle   Clayton   Jun 24, 1898
    Cards have been received announcing marriage of Miss Belle Bradney to
    Charles W. Maxwell at Delta, Colorado Thursday June 2nd 1898
BRADNEY, Miss Nellie   Jun 12, 1903
    See Moffett, James Renken
BRADY, Miss Anna   Mar 2, 1899
    See Winfield, Sidney
BRECKENRIDGE, Kittie   Local   Sep 12, 1896
    Kittie Breckenridge, of Kingston white cap fame, has sued her husband for
    divorce. She claims cruelty and desertion.
BREDETTE, H.P.   Mar 8, 1900
    See Beal, Miss Irene
BRIER, Fred   Feb 8, 1896
    See Stenhernburg, Miss Della
BRIERTON, Miss Emma   Jan 11, 1896
    See Noyes, Dr F.C.
BRIERTON, James F.   Local   Dec 5, 1901
    James F. Brierton, of Clayton, and Miss Ella Beckett, of Golden, were
    married at the home of brides parents on Thanksgiving Day.
BRINK, Oscar Bonney   Married   May 1, 1903
    Clipped from the Mt Sterling Republican and concerns a young man who at
    one time was employed in the New Era office. Invitations are out for
    marriage of Miss Ciella May Napier to Oscar Bonney Brink, both of
    Griggsville, at that city on Sunday April 26th. He was foreman of the
    Republican for almost a year and now holds similar position on the
    Pike County Times published in Pittsfield.
BROWN, Miss Ethel A.   Dec 25, 1903
    See Koontz, Ray L.
BROWN, Dr Harry   Neighborhood   Jul 31, 1897
    Telegram from Monmouth dated 19th inst.--Saturday Dr Harry Brown and Mrs
    Ella Welsh of Monmouth eloped. Dr left a young wife and daughter. Mrs
    Welsh leaves a husband. They are supposed to be on their way to California
                              (cont.)

Browning took with him his surgical instruments and $1,000 in a paper bag. Browning practiced for five years in New Windson, Mercer County.

BROWNING, Chas.   May 3, 1900
See Miller, Miss Margaret

BROWNING, Dr Harry   Jul 31, 1897
See Brown, Dr Harry

BRUNS, Miss Hattie   Feb 15, 1902
See Hashamyer, Edward

BRUNS, Henry   Local   Oct 16, 1903
At 10 AM last Sunday at Prairie Church, Henry Bruns and Miss Anna Heinecke were married by Rev Oetting. Groom is son of John Bruns and bride is daughter of August Heinecke Sr. Reception on Monday at home of brides parents. Will live Golden where groom has accepted a position in F.M. King's store.

BRUNS, Miss Lena   Apr 25, 1901
See Buhr, Men

BRUNS, Miss Maggie   Oct 14, 1904
See Flesner, Simon W.

BRUNS, William L.   Married   Jan 6, 1905
Married, William L. Bruns and Johanna Eigenberg at the home of the bride on Wednesday eve.

BUETEL, Frank   Camp Point   Dec 28, 1899
Frank Buetel and Miss Mary Hocamp were married at the home of the bride four miles south of town Tuesday of last week.

BUHR, Fred   Local   Jan 1, 1904
On Tuesday eve at Prairie Church, Fred Buhr and Miss Mary Haschemeyer were married by Rev Oetting. Bride is daughter of Chris Haschemeyer.

BUHR, Freda   Dec 2, 1904
See Behrens, Weert

BUHR, John   Local   May 19, 1905
John Buhr and Mattie Noftz, of Kellerville were married in Golden Tuesday AM. John has completed a new house on the farm north of town and is pretty well prepared to enjoy life.

BUHR, Miss Kate   Nov 13, 1897
See Juilfs, Dick

BUHR, Men   Local   Apr 25, 1901
Men Buhr, of LaPrairie and Miss Lena Bruns of Golden, were granted marriage license yesterday.

BULWAR, Bert   May 16, 1901
See Mikesel, Miss Chloe

BUNNELS, Walter F.   Local   Aug 28, 1903
Walter F. Bunnels, of Denver, Illinois and Edna A. Tarr, of Augusta, were married in Quincy on Wednesday.

BURKE, Miss Alta   May 25, 1899
See Oschner, Clarence

BURKE, Chas. L.   Elm Grove   Nov 7, 1901
"Too late for last week" Mr Chas. L. Burke and Miss Millie C. Robbins were quietly married at the Curry Hotel, Mt Sterling, Wednesday of last week by Judge Wallace.

BURKE, Miss Cora   Local   Sep 8, 1905
Miss Cora Burke and Harry Clark, of Mt Sterling, were married at the Methodist parsonage at Mt Sterling at 7:30 PM Tuesday. Will live Mt. Sterling where Mr Clark is in the harness business. The firm being Clark and O'Neal.

BURKE, E.L. and wife   Local   Oct 26, 1895
    Miss Flora Burke attended the wooden wedding of E.L. Burke and wife at
    Galesburg last week.
BURKE, Miss Jessie   Married   Jul 26, 1900
    At 5 PM July 22nd at the home of Mr and Mrs T.T. Burke of North East town-
    ship, occurred the marriage of their eldest daughter, Miss Jessie to
    Mr O.W. Alexander, of near Pine Grove, Illinois by Rev R.E. Mathis, groom
    is member of Horeb C.P. Church and bride is member of Elm Grove M.E. Churc
BURKE, Miss Lulu   Nov 21, 1902
    See Clark, Leon
BURKE, Miss Lulu   Elm Grove   Nov 14, 1902
    Miss Lulu Burke, of this locality and Mr Leon Clark will be married next
    Sunday eve at Elm Grove ME Church at 8 PM by Rev Evans, pastor of the
    church. Miss Burke is daughter of Thad T. Burke, of Golden and Mr Clark
    is son of Mr and Mrs T.J. Clark, of Quincy.
BURKE, Mr and Mrs Thad   Elm Grove   Dec 7, 1899
    Mr and Mrs Thad Burke attended the golden wedding of Mrs Burke's parents
    in Quincy on Thanksgiving Day.
BURMEISTER, John   Local   Nov 30, 1899
    Mr John Burmeister, of Quincy and Miss Annie Sartorius, of this place but
    who has made her home in Quincy for the past few months were married at
    the parsonage of the Quincy German ME Church Wednesday of last week.
    Will live Quincy.
BURNER, Miss Grace   Mar 27, 1902
    See Powell, Arthur
BURNETT, Miss Alta   Jan 3, 1901
    See Boyd, Robert
BURNS, Mr   Camp Point   Mar 13, 1897
    Mr Burns and Miss Cora Neuman were married Thursday eve at the Francis
    Hotel, the home of the bride. Will live Chicago.
BURNS, Miss Nannie   May 15, 1902
    See O'Dell, Justin
BURTON, John W.   Jun 26, 1903
    See Dorsett, Miss Bertha
BUSBOOM, Miss Dorothy   Local   Dec 22, 1905
    Cards are out announcing the wedding of Miss Dorothy Busboom, of Glenville
    Nebraska, to Chas. W. Walter of the same place. Wedding to occur on Dec-
    ember 24th it being also the brides birthday.
BUSBOOM, Heye T.   Local   Mar 13, 1903
    Heye T. Busboom, of Gifford, Ill and Mrs Lena Goldenstein, of Golden were
    married last week and will live near Gifford where Mr Burboom is a pros-
    perous farmer.
BUSBOOM, Ollie   Local   Feb 19, 1904
    Cards of invitation are out for wedding of Ollie Busboom and Miss Angie
    Zimmerman to take place at Wymore, Nebraska on Monday February 22nd.
BUSS, Miss Alice   Nov 27, 1903
    See Schoene, Oltman
BUSS, Miss Anna   January 1893   Jan 10, 1901
    See Franzen, Fred B.
BUSS, Miss Annie   Jan 22, 1898
    See Franzen, Fred
BUSS, Miss Emma   Local   Mar 24, 1905
    Wedding of Miss Emma Buss and Martin Fredericks, both of Filley, Nebraska
    is announced for Sunday March 26th. Both are well known in Golden. Miss
    Buss having lived just north of the village for some time.

BUSS, Miss Jennie   Local   Jun 29, 1899
  Married at the home of brides parents in LaPrairie, Illinois on Wednesday
  the 21st of June, Eilt Hendricks of this place and Miss Jennie Buss, of
  LaPrairie by Rev Dorrow, of this city. Miss Buss is daughter of Ralph
  Buss who for many years a prosperous merchant of Golden.
BUSS, John G.   Wedding   Apr 18, 1901
  Married Sunday at the East Side German Church, John G. Buss and Miss Bertha
  Duis by Rev Darrow just before the morning service. Ed Meyers and Miss
  Theda Duis acted as bridesman and groomsman. Miss Duis is daughter of
  Esq. W.D. Duis. Mr Buss is a son of Geo. W. Buss and is employed at
  Table Grove where they will live.
BUSS, John W.   Wedded   Apr 18, 1901
  At 7 last evening at the West Side German Lutheran Church, John W. Buss
  of this city and Miss Julia Fruehling, of LaPrairie were married by Rev
  Alpers. Miss Hattie Fruehling was maid of honor, J.J. Emminga was best
  man. Bridesmaids were, Misses Margaret Tansman, of Quincy and Marie
  Turbehn, of Peoria groomsmen were, Ehme Fruehling and Jacob Tenhoeff.
  Andy Harberts and Geo. Cassens served as ushers. Reception at home of
  brides parents near LaPrairie and another at the home of grooms parents,
  Mr and Mrs W.J. Buss. Will live in residence formerly occupied by
  Klaus Huisman.
BUSS, John W.   Local   May 2, 1901
  John W. Buss, of Golden, who was married last week was a soldier in the
  Spanish-American War. Monroe has his claim for pension. He is a bright
  and educated young man. "Saturday Review"
BUSS, Miss Katie   Local   Feb 16, 1899
  Miss Katie Buss, daughter of Mrs G.J. Buss, was married at the Prairie
  Church, Sunday to George A. Fritzen, of Beatrice, Nebraska by Rev Outing,
  pastor of the church. We do not know where they expect to live, Illinois
  or Nebraska.
BUSS, Miss Maggie   October 21, 1893   Jan 23, 1902
  See Eilts, John
Buss, Miss Mamie   Feb 22, 1896
  See Aden, George
BUSS, Miss Margaret   Apr 5, 1900
  See Janssen, George
BUSS, Miss Margaret   Apr 12, 1900
  See Janssen, George
BUSS, Miss Martha   Jan 30, 1897
  See Lanerts, Klaus
BUSS, Miss Martha G.   Jan 16, 1897
  See Lanerts, Klaas O.
BUTLER, Mr C.F.   Pine Grove   Aug 28, 1897
  The marriage of Mr C.F. Butler and Miss Dora Thompson, two of the groves
  popular young people occurred last week.
BUTLER, Frank   Elm Grove   Aug 28, 1897
  Mr Frank Butler and Miss Dora Thompson were married at La Belle, Missouri
  recently. Miss Thompson went there several weeks ago to visit her brother,
  Walter Thompson.
BYRONES, Archibal   Camp Point   Aug 30, 1900
  Archibal Byrones and Miss Susie Sherrick were married at the brides home
  last week at 4 o'clock by Elder Beadles.
CABELL, Mrs Anna   Jan 23, 1903
  Mrs Anna Cabell of Quincy was granted a divorce from her husband a few
  days ago, but they concluded to try it over again and were remarried the
  next day.

CAFFERY, James   Aug 14, 1897
    See Lanning, Miss Hattie
CAIN, Calvin   Augusta   Jun 24, 1898
    Married Wednesday eve June 15th Calvin Cain of Pulaski and Miss Blanche
    Dunn also of that place. Will live near Pulaski where he will teach
    next winter.
CAIN, Calvin   Union Items   Jun 24, 1898
    Ivin Black and family attended wedding of one of his old school mates,
    Calvin Cain, near Augusta last week.
CAIN, Calvin   Elm Grove   Jun 24, 1898
    Mr and Mrs Ira Reynolds attended wedding of Mr Calvin Cain and Miss Blanche
    Dunn near old Pulaski. "Cal" is one of our promising young men of "Poor
    old Carolina" and not without a hope of success in life.
CAIN, Charles O.   Married   Oct 17, 1896
    Married Saturday eve, two of Golden's citizens, Charles O. Cain and Miss
    Henrietta Cain by Esquire E.P. Thomas at his home in this city. Bride is
    eldest daughter of Mr and Mrs Warren Cain.
CAIN, Clarence   Local   Oct 2, 1903
    Clarence Cain and Miss Rena Mae Hopper, of Augusta, were married at
    Springfield, Wednesday.
CAIN, Elmer   Augusta   Oct 20, 1898
    Married Tuesday eve October 18th at home of brides sister, Mrs Emma Hough
    of this place. Mr Elmer Cain and Miss Pearl Dean, both of Pulaski at 8 PM
    by Rev F.B. Madden, pastor of the ME Church of this place. Will live at
    present with brides mother, Mrs Dean.
CAIN, Miss Henrietta   Oct 17, 1896
    See Cain, Charles O.
CAIN, Lewis L.   Married   Feb 26, 1904
    At 8 PM Monday at the ME parsonage, Lewis L. Cain and Miss Anna P. Matthews
    were married. Both are young people well known in Golden. Will live
    Galesburg where Mr Cain has a position with the C.B. & Q.
CAIN, Miss Orpha   Apr 20, 1899
    See Hillyer, Warren
CAIN, Orpha M.   La Prairie   Apr 27, 1899
    Last Sunday at 7 PM at the home of Mr and Mrs Philip Cain of Northeast
    township occurred the marriage of their daughter, Orpha M. to Dr Warren
    E. Hillyer of Huntsville, Illinois by Rev R.E. Mathis.
CALDWELL, Sadie   May 1, 1897
    See Getts, Charlie
CALKINS, Miss Effie   Dec 23, 1904
    See Koontz, Charles
CALLAHAN, Miss Frances   Jun 10, 1904
    See Nations, Dr Guy
CALLAHAN, Matthew Wesley   Overlooked Wedding   Jul 1, 1904
    By some oversight, no mention was made last week of the marriage in Quincy
    on the 15th inst, of Matthew Wesley Callahan and Mrs Anna Lear. They left
    for St Louis and spent a few days at the exposition before settling down.
    "Camp Point Journal"
CALLAHAN, Miss Mildred Blanche   Mar 24, 1905
    See Ihrig, John H.
CAMPBELL, Charles O.   York Neck   Jan 4, 1899
    Mr and Mrs John Beer attended the wedding of Charles O. Campbell and Miss
    Sadie Hirons, of Clayton, New Years evening.
CAMPBELL, Miss Pearl   Dec 6, 1900
    See Cox, Perry

CANNON, Miss   Dec 7, 1899
  See Hostetter, Alvin
CANNON, Miss Pearl   Dec 7, 1899
  See Hostetter, Alvin
CANTRELL, Miss Laura   Wedding   May 9, 1896
  Miss Laura Cantrell of Camp Point township was married at Quincy at 1 PM
  Sunday to Henry Ohnemus of 1121 Chestnut St. Quincy. She has been living
  at Adam Shake's, of this township. Will live Quincy.
CARLIN, Miss Hattie B.   Wedding Bells   Jan 17, 1901
  Marriage of Miss Hattie B. Carlin, only daughter of Mr and Mrs Wm Carlin,
  Sr. to Mr R.M. Beckett, of Camp Point, Illinois was solemnized at the
  home of the birde, Thursday eve, January 10. Ceremony, according to the
  Discipline of the ME Church, was performed by Rev Chas. Wehrman, of
  Golden in presence of relatives and a few of brides intimate friends.
  Wedding march played by Mrs Rev Wehrman and Miss Pearl Garner assisted in
  receiving the guests. Bride is an accomplished musician, a teacher in
  the Hebron ME Sunday School. Groom is a stalwart young farmer, whose
  family for generations have resided in this neighborhood.
CARLIN, J.T.   Local   Jun 13, 1901
  Monday afternoon at the Lamar Hotel in Quincy, J.T. Carlin, of Abingdon and
  Mrs Lizzie Black, of Monmouth, were married by Rev McKernon of this place.
  Mr Carlin is a brother of Wm Carlin Sr. Both bride and groom have arrived
  at a good sensible age.
CARLIN, James T.   Married   Jun 13, 1901
  At theHotel Lamar, Quincy, Illinois June 10th the marriage ceremony was
  performed for, Mr James T. Carlin, of Abingdon, Illinois and Mrs Mary
  Elizabeth Black, of Monmouth, Illinois by Rev T.A. McKernon, of Golden,
  Illinois. Miss Hazel Potter, Monmouth, Miss Sadie Wallace, Mrs Mary
  E.S. McKernon and Mr T. Carlin from Golden and Mr Bowls from Quincy were
  present. Supper was served at the hotel. Will live at Abingdon, Ill.
CARLIN, Miss Nellie   June 23, 1894   Jul 24, 1902
  See Lambert, Dr.
CARLIN, Tom   5 Years Ago   Oct 16, 1897
  Tom Carlin and Miss Lou Wallace were married.
CARLIN, Wm F.   Local   Mar 13, 1902
  Not mentioned last week was the marriage of Wm F. Carlin and Perlia Garner,
  of Clayton at the home of Rev Wehrman in this village.
CARNAHAN, Mildred   Jan 1, 1898
  See Williams, Wilbur L.
CARPER, Melvin   Augusta   Feb 7, 1901
  Melvin Carper and May Jackson will be married Wednesday eve at the home
  of the brides parents, five miles northwest of Augusta.
CARSTEENS, Chris   Local   Nov 14, 1902
  Chris Carsteens and wife departed for Beatrice, Nebraska, Tuesday, where
  they will reside. The couple married at Prairie Church two weeks ago.
  Bride was formerly Miss Lena Post and is a daughter of Gerd Post, who
  lives southeast of town. Groom is a Nebraska product.
CARSTINS, Dick   Historical   Apr 18, 1901
  March 18, 1893 Dick Carstins and Mary Flesner were licensed to wed.
CARTER, David W. and William T.   Local   Oct 21, 1904
  Double wedding occurred at a neighboring village on Thursday eve of last
  week. Rev W.T. Evans was a ambrose holding a meeting that eve and after
  services was invited to perform the ceremony by which Mr David W. Carter
  and Miss Pearl Jones and Mr William T. Carter and Miss Ora L. Matheny, of
  Augusta became members of the universal order of the happy married people.

CASSENS, George   Local   Aug 28, 1903
    Married last Saturday eve at 8 PM at East Side Church by Rev Dorrow,
    George Cassens and Miss Catherine Franzen, both of this village.
    Reception Sunday at home of brides parents, Mr and Mrs Harm Franzen.
    Groom is son of Mrs F. Cassens, of this village.
CASSENS, Wm   8 Years Ago   Jul 4, 1901
    June 17, 1893 Wm Cassens and Grace Buss were married.
CASTLE, Harry   Camp Point   Mar 15, 1900
    Harry Castle and Miss Emma Kiekehovel were married Thursday eve of last
    week. They had a neat cottage all furnished and ceremony was performed
    at their own home.
CASTLE, Joseph   Camp Point   Oct 5, 1899
    Joseph Castle and Miss Kate Sawin were married last Thursday eve at their
    own home, which was a gift to them by Mrs Mattie Mileham, sister of the
    groom.
CASTLE, Richard   Camp Point   Apr 3, 1902
    Wedding of Richard Castle and Miss Jessie Hendricks took place at the
    brides home Wednesday eve. Elder Webb performed the ceremony. Will
    live Kewanee.
CASTLE, Richard   Camp Point   Mar 27, 1902
    Cards are out announcing wedding of Richard Castle and Miss Jessie
    Hendricks Thursday of this week.
CATE, Miss Nona   Jan 26, 1899
    See Childs, Arthur
CHAMBERS, F.L. (Frank)   Augusta   Jan 3, 1901
    By the Macomb papers we learn that a marriage license has been issued to
    F.L. Chambers and Florence G. Wilson, both of Blandinsville, and before
    this no doubt are happily married. Groom is our Frank Chambers son of
    A. Chambers. Was born and raised in Augusta and for many years was the
    efficient clerk at the Boston Clothing store. He now has charge of the
    Blandinsville Clothing Company bride for several years has been one of the
    teachers in the schools of her home town.
CHAMP, Mr   Local   Apr 10, 1897
    A young man named Champ, working near Littleton, decided he needed a wife.
    He called on Miss Stambough Friday night and laid his proposition before
    her. Saturday AM he sent to Rushville for the marriage license and to
    Littleton for a preacher and they were married Saturday eve. Entire
    courtship took place in less than 24 hours.
CHAMPION, Homer   Bethel   Sep 1, 1898
    Homer Champion and Miss Eva Alexander were married at Augusta Wednesday.
CHAMPION, Homer   Sep 1, 1898
    See Alexander, Miss Eva
CHAPMAN, Miss Cleora   Local   Jun 27, 1901
    Fargo Forum & Republican: The nuptials of Miss Cleora Chapman and Lewis E.
    Whray took place Tuesday eve at the home of the bride, 812 4th Ave. N. by
    Rev H.K. Gebhart, pastor of the English Lutheran Church. Wedding guests
    were relatives of bride and groom. Mr Whray is a Western Union Telegraph
    operator in the local office. Bride has been connected with same office
    for some time.
CHILDS, Arthur   Camp Point   Jan 26, 1899
    Arthur Childs and Miss Nona Cate were married Thursday eve, January 19th by
    Rev Porter, they will go to housekeeping at once in Mr Childs elegant
    home at the east end of School Street.
CHINN, Miss Jessie   Jan 30, 1903
    See Omer, Cornelius S.

CLARE, Moses   Neighborhood   May 1, 1897
    A month or two ago Moses Clare was married to a Clayton lady. Last Satur-
    day his wife applied for a divorce and the divorce was granted. "Barry Adage"
CLARK, Miss Dora E.   May 27, 1904
    See Younglove, James W.
CLARK, Eva   Nov 6, 1903
    See Feril, Lee
CLARK, Frank   Local   Oct 2, 1903
    Frank Clark and Mrs Etta Hazlett, of Quincy were married this week.
CLARK, Harry   Sep 8, 1905
    See Burke, Miss Cora
CLARK, Jesse   Local   Sep 25, 1903
    Jesse Clark, of Bushnell and Miss Cornie Hostetter, of Camp Point were
    married last Sunday in Quincy. They left Monday for Bushnell, where they
    will live. Groom has relatives living east of Golden.
CLARK, Mr Leon   Nov 14, 1902
    See Burke, Miss Lulu
CLARK, Leon   Wedding   Nov 21, 1902
    Wedding at Elm Grove Church Sunday afternoon, Leon Clark, of Mt Sterling
    and Miss Lulu Burke, of Elm Grove at 4 PM just after the regular after-
    noon services by Rev W.T. Evans. Miss Alta Burke played the wedding
    march. Reception at home of brides sister, Mrs O.W. Alexander. Groom
    is son of T.J. Clark of Quincy and is a prosperous young farmer and is
    connnected with some of the best known families in Brown County. Bride
    is daughter of T.T. Burke of Golden.
CLARK, Miss Mabel Fern   Jun 3, 1904
    See Sealock, C.R.
CLARK, N.H.   Wedding Anniversary   Nov 22, 1900
    45th wedding anniversary of N.H. Clark and wife, of Pine Grove was cele-
    brated by children and friends last Thursday. They have lived in same
    neighborhood during nearly all of their married life and past 27 years in
    same house. They are parents of 8 children, 6 of whom were present from a
    distance were sons, Henry, of Dallas City, J.B. of Augusta and their
    daughter Mrs Maggie Laughlin, of Unionville, Missouri and Mrs Nancy Wells
    and Mrs Ollie Robertson of Bowen.
CLARKSTON, Josie   Pine Grove   May 6, 1898
    Josie Clarkston received a divorce at court last Tuesday.
COATS, Paul   La Prairie   Dec 29, 1905
    Mr Paul Coats and Miss Flora Sylvester left Saturday for Galesburg to be
    married, from there they go to Chicago where they expect to make their
    future home.
COCKERN, John S.   Local   Jul 8, 1898
    On Tuesday eve of last week occurred the marriage of Mr John S. Cockern,
    editor of the Carthage Journal, to Miss Emily M. Johnson of the same city.
CODDINGTON, Miss Della   Jul 5, 1900
    See Tuggle, Thomas
COFFIELD, Louis   Oakwood   Feb 27, 1902
    Geo. Giddings, wife and daughter attended the wedding of Louis Coffield
    last week.
COLEMAN, Gabe   Camp Point   Apr 20, 1899
    Supplement   Gabe Coleman says the wedding of him and Miss Howe, of Iowa
    is postponed until June. We'll see.
COLEMAN, Gabe   Camp Point   Mar 7, 1901
    Gabe Coleman and Mary Read were married by Justice Riley at his home
    Thursday eve.

CONNER, James   Camp Point   Oct 23, 1897
    James Conner and Miss Berdie Earl were married at the home of the bride
    Monday eve. Will live Galesburg. Groom works as brakeman on the CB & Q.
COOK, Thomas   Local   May 8, 1903
    Marriage license issued to Thomas Cook, of Chatten, and Miss Amanda Eweing
    of Loraine last Saturday.
CORDUM, Mrs Reka   Oct 17, 1902
    See Detmers, Herman
CORLETT, Miss Fannie   Nov 21, 1901
    See Ferguson, Frank
COSIT, Oliver   York Neck   Mar 16, 1899
    Married Wednesday, Oliver Cosit and Jennie Mathews.
COSTIGAN, James   Local   Dec 25, 1903
    Mrs W.D. Duis and daughter Clara, have to go to Springfield to attend
    wedding of James Costigan and Miss Ella Weities, which will occur on De-
    cember 30th.
COURTNEY, Mrs   Nov 2, 1899
    See Gibney, Michael
COURTNEY, Mrs Matilda   Feb 9, 1899
    See Lantice, William
COX, Miss Florence   May 15, 1903
    See Winfield, George
COX, Perry   Augusta   Dec 6, 1900
    Perry Cox and Miss Pearl Campbell were married at the office of Judge Alle
    in Quincy last Wednesday. Returned that evening and went immediately to
    their home in northeast part of town.
CRABBIE, Miss Annie   Jun 14, 1900
    See Lemmon, Asabel
CRAIG, George   Local   Jan 23, 1903
    Marriage license issued Wednesday to George Craig, of Loraine and Sarah C.
    Irvin, of Mendon.
CRAIG, Wesley   Augusta   Nov 15, 1900
    Wednesday eve of this week occurred the wedding of Wesley Craig, of St
    Louis, to Miss Christa Wessels, daughter of Mr and Mrs Bert Wessels, of
    1428 State St. Quincy at the home of bride.
CRAVEN, Mr and Mrs John   Local   Aug 1, 1896
    Mrs Fred Boger attended anniversary of wedding of Mr and Mrs John Craven
    recently.
CRAVER, Miss Carrie   Mar 20, 1903
    See Hostetter, Clarence
CREEL, T.J.   Mar 16, 1899
    See Smith, Ruth
CROMWELL, Thad   La Prairie   Feb 15, 1900
    On Wednesday at the home of Jack Pierce in Quincy occurred the wedding of
    Thad Cromwell and Miss Sadie Pierce. Will live on a farm 2½ miles from
    Clayton.
CRONIN, Mr   Jan 1, 1898
    See Stiffy, Miss Susan
CROOK, John   Elm Grove   Sep 5, 1901
    Mr John Crook and Miss Belle Paxton were married Wednesday eve at the home
    of John Alexander. Miss Paxton is s sister of Mrs John Alexander.
CROOK, John A.   Local   Sep 5, 1901
    John A. Crook, of Golden and Belle Paxton, of La Prairie, were licensed to
    wed Tuesday.

CROSSLAND, Jacob   February 4, 1893   Jan 31. 1901
    February 4--Jacob Crossland and Miss Clara VanBrunt, of Bowen were married.
CRUM, Miss Cora   Feb 1, 1900
    See Rice, J.H.
CUBBAGE, Miss Lutrecia   Feb 23, 1899
    See Shriver, James
CUBBAGE, Theresa   Married   Feb 23, 1899
    Married at the home of Mr and Mrs J.H. Cubbage near Loraine, on Wednesday
    at 6 PM February 15th, their daughter, Theresa, to James Shriver. Wedding
    march played by Miss Alma Bottorf. Ceremony performed by Mr Reece. Will
    live near Loraine. Reception held at home of B.F. Shriver and wife next
    day.
CUMMINGS, Tom   Camp Point   May 30, 1901
    Tom Cummings and Miss Rosa Bartells were married at the brides home on
    Wednesday eve of last week.
CUNNINGHAM, Fred   Local   Sep 1, 1898
    Today will occur the wedding of Fred Cunningham and Miss Emma Wallace at
    the brides home in this city.
CUNNINGHAM, Fred   Married   Sep 8, 1898
    Mr Fred Cunningham and Miss Emma A. Wallace were married at her home last
    Thursday eve at 7 by Rev M.W. Lorimer. Will live here. Bride was born
    near Golden and always lived within four miles of town.
CURRY, Miss Florence   Dec 7, 1899
    See DeMoss, James E.
CURRY, Miss Laura   December 2, 1893   Feb 6, 1902
    See Seaton, Tom
CUTTER, Miss Flora May   Dec 11, 1903
    See Boger, Arthur C.
CYZENSE, Prof. Frank   Local   Apr 29, 1898
    Prof. Frank Cyzense and Miss Martha Peil were married at the home of brides
    mother Tuesday eve by Rev Dorrow of the East Side German Church.
DACE, Mr I.B.   Sep 15, 1905
    See Schoneman, Miss Eureka
DAUGHERTY, John M. and Ella   Miserable Married Men   Jul 4, 1896
    Divorce case of John M. Daugherty vs Ella Daugherty, rule has been entered
    for the defendent to answer by Friday.
DAVIS, Miss Eva   Married   Mar 18, 1904
    On Wednesday at 5:30 PM at home of brides parents, Mr and Mrs George Davis,
    occurred the wedding of Miss Eva Davis to Bruce Roberts, by Rev Hartley.
    Groom is a farmer of Houston township.
DAVIS, George   Pea Ridge   Mar 21, 1901
    Mr George Davis, of Damon, and Miss Alta Dunbar were married last week.
DAVIS, Miss Laura Bell   May 19, 1905
    Wedding at Clayton Sunday afternoon at the home of Mr Abraham Davis and
    wife, parents of the young lady to the matrimonial alliance, Miss Laura
    Bell Davis to Mr John W. Jones, who has his home over in Schuyler County
    near Camden. Ceremony performed by L.L. Dodd, Esq. Will live in vicinity
    of Camden, where Mr Jones has employment as a machinist.
DAVIS, Miss Margaret E.   Jun 14, 1900
    See Siebert, Matthew M.
DAVIS, Mrs Nancy   Bowen   Mar 28, 1896
    Married Sunday eve 5:30 at her own residence, Mrs Nancy Davis to James Ball
    by Rev Nay.
DAVIS, Robert   Camp Point   Feb 8, 1896
    Robert Davis and Miss Rebecca White were married Sunday eve.

DAWSON, Mrs Maggie   Jul 24, 1902
   See Bennett, Alvin
DEAN, Miss Pearl   Oct 20, 1898
   See Cain, Elmer
DEANE, Alfred G.   Local   Nov 20, 1903
   Alfred G. Deane, of Pine Grove, and Miss Cecil Dora Woods, of Huntsville,
   were married this week.
DEANE, Miss Bessie   Feb 8, 1900
   See Dutton, J.H.
DECKER, Andrew F.   Local   Feb 6, 1902
   Andrew F. Decker, of Camp Point, and Hattie B. Hudson, of Loraine, were
   married last week.
DEGROOT, Miss Bertha   Jun 12, 1902
   See Roberts, Dr R.B.
DEGROOT, John B.   Elm Grove   Oct 26, 1895
   John B. De Groot and Mrs Eads were married recently, but the exact time
   and place is not known.
DEGROOT, Maude   Dec 22, 1898
   See Laughlin, Arthur
DEHAVEN, Hattie   Apr 12, 1900
   See Omer, Pete
DEHAVEN, Will   Camp Point   Dec 1, 1898
   Will Dehaven and Miss Florence Joseph were married at the home of the
   bride Thursday November 24th by Rev Dillen.
DEJEAN, C.B.   Camp Point   Oct 16, 1897
   Elder O. Dilley officiated at the marriage of C.B. DeJean to Miss Minnie
   Thompson, Wednesday at Coatsburg.
DEJEAN, Clarence B.   Local   Oct 9, 1897
   Clarence B. DeJean recently sold his Coatsburg Review and he has now taken
   himself a wife. His wife was Miss Minnie Thompson, of that place.
DEMOSS, Miss Bertie   Clayton   Jan 1, 1898
   To be married Tuesday at the home of John DeMoss, west of town, Miss Bertie
   DeMoss and Charles Peacock of Kingston.
DEMOSS, James E.   Local   Dec 7, 1899
   Mr and Mrs V.G. Manlove received invitation yesterday to attend wedding of
   Mrs Manlove's nephew, James E. DeMoss, of Clayton to Miss Florence Curry.
   Wedding will take place December 21st at high noon.
DENNY, Miss May   Jan 25, 1900
   See Thompson, Arthur
DETMERS, Chas. H.   Married   May 15, 1897
   Chas. H. Detmers and Miss Mary Duden, two young german citizens of ours
   were married at the homeof Jas. F. Smith.Sunday at 5 PM by Rev P. Slagle.
   Mr Detmers is clerk at Boger's store. Will live in W.D. Duis' house near
   Keller's shop.
DETMERS, Christopher H.   8 Years Ago   Jul 4, 1901
   May 27, 1893 Christopher H. Detmers and Anna C. Franzen were married at
   Bentley.
DETMERS, George   5 Years Ago   Feb 20, 1897
   George Detmers and Miss Nettie Jacobs, were married by Rev Dorrow.
DETMERS, Herman   Local   Oct 17, 1902
   Henry Detmers was visited last week by his cousin, Herman Detmers and wife.
   Mrs Detmers was formerly Mrs Reka Cordum of Gillipsie, Illinois. They were
   married by a short time ago and were on their bridal tour. Mr Setmers is
   very prominent in his home city, Alton.

DETMERS, Miss Tena   Married   Jan 8, 1898
   Sunday AM just before preaching service at the East Side German Church,
   occurred the marriage of Miss Tena Detmers to Rank O. Lanerts by Rev
   Darrow bride is daughter of townsman Henry Detmers. Groom was born and
   raised here.
DICKHUT, Clarence   Camp Point   May 31, 1900
   Married in Quincy last Wednesday, Clarence Dickhut to Miss Cora Beckett.
   Bride is of Camp Point. Groom is of Fowler. Will live Fowler after
   June 1st.
DONLEY, Anderson   York Neck   Mar 16, 1899
   Married Wednesday, Anderson Donley of Big Neck and Nora Maynard, of
   Primrose.
DONLEY, Jack   Local   Mar 9, 1899
   As we go to press we learn of marriage of Jack Donley and Miss Fairy
   Downing, daughter of townsman Will Downing at the home of brides parents
   at 6 PM yesterday. Will live on R.E. Downing's farm near Chatten.
DONLEY, Lige   York Neck   Mar 16, 1899
   Married Wednesday, Lige Donley and Fairy Downing, of Golden.
DONLEY, Miss Mary   May 22, 1903
   See Poling, William B.
DONLEY, Thomas   Big Neck   Mar 2, 1899
   Married in Camp Point, February 22, Mr Thomas Donley and Miss Myra West.
   They moved Friday to the Rezin Downing farm now owned by Alex Calahan,
   of Camp Point.
DONLEY, Thomas   York Neck   Mar 2, 1899
   Married, Thomas Donley and Miss Myra West, both of Big Neck last week.
DORAN, Wm   Local   Jan 2, 1902
   Wm Doran, of Quincy, was too timid to stand up and be married. He was only
   38 years old and extreme youth may be offered as an excuse.
DOREN, Harm   Local   Mar 31, 1905
   Harm Doren and Miss Margaret Stubbens were married at the Luther Memorial
   Church parsonage at Quincy Wednesday afternoon at 3 by Rev E.P. Scheuler
   and witnessed by Mr and Mrs George Tieken of Coatsburg. Will live Golden.
DORSETT, Miss Bertha   Married   Jun 26, 1903
   Married at the home of J.C. Dorsett at 8 PM Wednesday, May 20th, Miss Bertha,
   only daughter of J.C. and Mary Dorsett, of Avon township, to Mr John W.
   Burton, of Palestine township. Mr Burton is a farmer. His father died
   10 or 11 years ago and he has largely supported family since. Elder J.M.
   Via, pastor of the Wellington Baptist Church said words to make them man
   and wife. Item clipped from May 27th issue of a Wellington, Kan. newspaper.
DORSEY, Miss Margaret   Dec 25, 1903
   See Spears, John
DORSEY, Pearl   Augusta   Jun 28, 1900
   Last Wednesday AM at the home of Joseph Dorsey and wife, of Carthage,
   occurred the marriage of their daughter, Pearl to Ed Hoch by Rev C.J.
   Schofield. Mr and Mrs Dorsey moved from Augusta to Carthage three years
   ago. Groom is in the book and stationary business in Carthage.
DOWING, Fairy   Mar 16, 1899
   See Donley, Lige
DOWNING, Albert   Big Neck   Oct 20, 1898
   Albert Downing is married and settled down to hard study at medical school
   at Keokuk.
DOWNING, Miss Bertha   Sep 15, 1898
   See Edmunds, Roe
DOWNING, Miss Eva   Jan 8, 1904
   See Miller, Ray

DOWNING, Miss Fairy   Mar 9, 1899
   See Donley, Jack
DOWNING, Miss Harriet E.   Feb 19, 1898
   See Poling, Eugene P.
DOWNING, Miss Hattie   Aug 22, 1892
   See Lance, Joe
DOWNING, James   Local   Nov 25, 1904
   James Downing, of Camp Point and Miss Mabel Smurr, of Springfield were
   married Wednesday the 16th at Springfield.
DOWNING, Warren H.   Wedding   Dec 27, 1900
   Thursday December 20, 1900 at the home of brides parents, the Rev Chas.
   Wehrman united in marriage Warren H. Downing and Neva Myrtle McClintock
   at 6 PM present from a distance were: Mr and Mrs J. Henshaw of Shelbina,
   Missouri, Mr and Mrs J.R. Gray, Quincy, Illinois, Mrs N.E. Potter and
   daughter of Windsor, Illinois and Misses Edith and Ethel Smith of Camp
   Point. Reception at home of grooms mother at 12 Friday. Will live on his
   farm two miles northwest of Golden after January 15, 1901
DUDEN, Miss Mary   May 15, 1897
   See Detmers, Chas. H.
DUFF, Rev James M.   Dec 22, 1898
   See Huff, Mrs Laura E.
DUFF, Rev James M.   Wedding Bells   Dec 22, 1898
   Married this week, Rev James M. Duff of Literberry, Illinois to Mrs Laura E
   Huff at home of brides mother, Mrs M.J. Schwartz Wednesday at 5 PM. Mrs
   Huff is daughter of the late John G. Schwartz. Will live Literberry.
DUIS, Miss Bertha   Apr 18, 1901
   See Buss, John G.
DUIS, Miss Dora   Nov 13, 1897
   See Beckett, Harry I.
DUIS, Miss Lena   Local   May 27, 1898
   Friends have received invitation to marriage of Miss Lena Duis and Alva
   Kelley which will take place at Carthage June 1st.
DUIS, Miss Lena   Married in Carthage   Jun 10, 1898
   Last Wednesday June 1st occurred the marriage , in Carthage, of Miss Lena
   Duis and Alfonzo Kelley at 8 by Dr Hyde. Mr Kelley is practicing law in
   Carthage.
DUIS, Miss Theda   Oct 24, 1901
   See Meyer, Edward H.
DUIS, Theda Methea   Oct 31, 1901
   See Meyer, Edward H.
DUMNEY, Herbert C.   Local   Jun 8, 1899
   Marriage license issued to Herbert C. Dumney, of Omaha and Katherine S.
   Blood of Camp Point this week.
DUNANT, Miss Tennie Esther   Apr 1, 1904
   See McCoy, Ralph O.
DUNBAR, Miss Alta   Mar 21, 1901
   See Davis, George
DUNLAP, Iris M.   Apr 17, 1902
   See Kipp, Edward
DUNLAP, Miss Mabel   Local   Oct 14, 1904
   Miss Mabel Dunlap, of Bowen, Illinois and Enoch Fleming, also of Bowen,
   were married Wednesday last at the home of brides sister, Mrs Edward Kipp,
   816 N. Leavitt St, Chicago. Will live Bowen.
DUNN, Miss Blanche   Jun 24, 1898
   See Cain, Calvin

DUTTON, Miss Bertie   Horeb   Feb 28, 1901
   Cards are out announcing the marriage of Miss Bertie Dutton to Wm Stover
   at 6:30 PM Thursday.
DUTTON, Bertie   Pine Grove   Mar 7, 1901
   Bertie Dutton and Wm Stover were married at the home of bride Thursday,
   February 28th at 6:30 PM by Rev W.W. Henry of La Prairie.
DUTTON, Prof. Frank F.   Elm Grove   Jul 12, 1900
   Prof. Frank F. Dutton, who was married to Miss Catherine Stevens at the home
   of brides parents in Trenton, New Jersey came west to spend the honeymoon.
   Arrived June 27th at the home of his parents, Mr and Mrs J.P. Dutton where
   there was a reception by the parents and sisters and about 40 guests. Will
   return to Trenton where Mr Dutton will resume his duties as a teacher in
   penmanship.
DUTTON, J.H.   Pine Grove   Feb 8, 1900
   J.H. Dutton and Miss Bessie Deane were married at the home of the brides
   mother, last Wednesday at 6 PM.
DWIRE, Miss Jennie   Jan 30, 1902
   See Ward, Otho
DYER, Edward   Mar 16, 1899
   See Smith, Ruth
EADS, <u>Mrs</u>   Oct 26, 1895
   See DeGroot, John B.
EARL, Miss Berdie   Oct 23, 1897
   See Conner, James
EARY, Ray   Big Neck   Oct 20, 1905
   Mr Ray Eary and Miss Neva Ketchum were married Wednesday of last week. When
   they arrived home from Quincy a large number were at the depot where they
   were showered with rice.
EATON, Miss Dora   Elm Grove   Dec 22, 1898
   Cards are out for wedding of Miss Dora Eaton to Wilson Smith, December 22.
EATON, Miss Dora   Wedding Bells   Dec 22, 1898
   Thursday December 22nd at the residence of the brides <u>parents</u>, Mr and Mrs
   R.G. Pettijohn occured the marriage of their daughter Miss Dora Eaton to
   Mr Wilson Smith by Rev Mathis, of LaPrairie. Bridesmaids were Miss Grace
   Robbins and Mrs Chas Marsh while P.L. Alexander and Chas. Marsh acted as
   groomsmen.
EATON, Wm   Nov 14, 1896
   See McDonald, Mabel
EBER, Alfred L.   Local   Dec 4, 1903
   Alfred L. Eber and Miss Nina Trout, of Camp Point were married this week.
EBER, Miss Minnie   Mar 10, 1905
   See Flesner, Gerhard W.
ECKHOFF, Miss Mattie   May 3, 1900
   See Jurgens, John Jr.
ECKLES, Tom   From old New Era's   Jul 24, 1902
   June 16, 1894 Tom Eckles and Miss Blanche Kern were married.
EDMUNDS, James   Good Story Spoiled   Oct 9, 1897
   March 18, 1882, James Edmunds, of Carthage, Ill and Cora M. Allen of Barry,
   Ill were granted license to wed and were married same day by Rev W.F.
   Short. Groom was 10 days under age and carried a written consent signed
   by his father. For some reason the couple left the time and place of their
   marriage a secret and when they died a few years ago, leaving 1 daughter no
   one knew they married. Child is 14 years old and both of her parents are
   dead and she is the only direct heir to her grandfathers estate of $80,000.
   The other heirs claim her parents were never married. Today the county

clerk's office found the record and license to marriage, proving con-
clusively that the daughter of James Edmunds is right heir to the large
estate.
Barry Adage remarks: The above is a nice story and the only thing wrong
with it is that it is a hoax. Judge Edmunds has no $80,000 to leave if
he were dead, there is no child such as mentioned and neither James
Edmunds nor Mrs Cora Edmunds are dead.

EDMUNDS, Roe   Clayton   Sep 15, 1898
Mr Roe Edmunds, of this city, and Miss Bertha Downing, daughter of Mr
J.E. Downing deceased, were married at the parental home in Camp Point
township 8 PM Wednesday by Rev Dr Scott of Quincy.

EELLS, Miss Grace   Local   Jun 17, 1898
Mrs R.J. McCray and Miss Maude Seaton attended wedding of Miss Grace Eells
at Bowen on Wednesday.

EELLS, Miss Grace   Local   Jun 24, 1898
Miss Grace Eells and Oscar Gragg were married in Bowen Wednesday June 18th
Mr Gragg is employed at Crain's Clothing store in Augusta.

EELLS, Miss Grace   Jun 24, 1898
See Gragg, Oscar O.

EGGAN, Miss Anna   Mar 14, 1896
See Flessner, W.H.

EGGEN, Carl   Local   Dec 20, 1902
At the Prairie Church last Sunday two excellent young people, Carl Eggen
and Miss Clara Oetting were married. Went to housekeeping at once.

EHNEN, Aime   Double Wedding   Mar 27, 1897
Sunday occurred the marriage of four of Goldens young people, Chris
Fredericks and Miss Mary Ehnen and Aime Ehnen and Miss Hannah Weyen at the
East Side Lutheran Church by Rev Dorrow.

EHNEN, Miss Annie   Apr 17, 1897
See Herron, Henry

EHNEN, Miss Mary   Mar 27, 1897
See Fredericks, Chris

EIGENBERG, Miss Alvina V.   Jun 3, 1904
See Utesch, Rev John H.

EIGENBERG, Miss Avina V.   May 27, 1904
See Utesch, Rev John H.

EIGENBERG, Miss Emma   Mar 1, 1900
See Janssen, Albertus

EIGENBERG, Johanna   Jan 6, 1905
See Bruns, William L.

EIGENBERG, Miss Margaret   Nov 18, 1904
See Gronewold, William

EIGENBERG, Margaret   Dec 2, 1904
See Gronowold, William

EIGENBURG, Miss Minnie   Jan 11, 1900
See Harberts, Jurgen H.

EILERS, Nickles   Local   Nov 23, 1899
Nickles Eilers, of LaPrairie and Anna Osterman, of Golden were licensed to
wed last week. It is reported that the ceremony took place last evening.

EILTS, John   Review   Jan 23, 1902
October 21, 1893 John Eilts and Miss Maggie Buss were married.

ELLIOT, Helen A.   Jun 20, 1896
See Levy, Joseph

ELLIS, Ben F.   Augusta   Nov 22, 1900
Sunday eve at 7:30 Ben F. Ellis and Cora L. Farlow were married at home
of brides parents by Rev John Stahl. Bride was daughter of J. Farlow and
groom is member of the grocer firm of Rogon & Ellis & Augusta.

EMERY, Olin   Local   Oct 24, 1896
  Olin Emery, editor of the Augusta Eagle, and Miss Daisy Leach, of that place
  were married in Quincy last week.
ESHOM, Mr Savil H.   Nov 23, 1895
  See McClintock, Miss Jennie
EWEING, Miss Amanda   May 8, 1903
  See Cook, Tomas
EWEN, Lizzie   Mar 13, 1903
  See Goldenstein, Oltman W.
EWEN, Miss Lizzie M.   Mar 20, 1903
  See Goldenstein, Oltman W.
EYMAN, Walter   Mar 13, 1902
  See Ross, Miss Effie
EYMAN, Walter   Mar 13, 1902
  See Ross, Effie
FARLOW, Cora L.   Nov 22, 1900
  See Ellis, Ben F.
FARLOW, Mattie   May 1, 1897
  See Henry, Hez
FARLOW, Miss Mattie   Apr 24, 1897
  See Henry, Hez G.
FARLOW, Miss Nell   Jan 12, 1899
  See Pope, Sam
FELSMAN, Albert   February 1893   Feb 21, 1901
  February 18 Albert Felsman, of Coatsburg, and Miss Mary Acklem were
  married.
FERGUSON, F.E.   Augusta   Jun 28, 1900
  F.E. Ferguson, son of Elder Ferguson and wife, and Miss Beulah Ruggles,
  of Peoria were married at the home of brides parents last Tuesday at 11 AM
  the father of the groom officiating. Will live Indianapolis.
FERGUSON, Frank   Augusta   Nov 21, 1901
  Invitations have been received here to the wedding of Frank Ferguson and
  Miss Fannie Corlett which will take place at Rockford, Wednesday November
  27th. Mr Ferguson is a son of Elder Ferguson of this place.
FERIL, Lee   Local   Nov 6, 1903
  A marriage license was issued Monday to Lee Feril, of Bowen and Eva Clark,
  of Loraine.
FERMAN, Arthur   Aug 7, 1897
  See Jacobs, Miss Alta
FERRICK, Charlie   Jun 20, 1901
  See Tribune, Miss Lucy
FERRIS, John   Jan 2, 1897
  John Ferris, age 34 and Riddie Pillars, 13 yrs. of age were married last
  week in Quincy.
FIERICHS, Pada   May 29, 1897
  See Sieper, John
FINGERHIM, Gotleb   Columbus   Mar 13, 1897
  Marriage of Gotleb Fingerhim to Miss Lizzie Stoeszel occurred Monday.
FINK, Andreas H.   Local   Nov 9, 1899
  Last Friday Andreas H. Fink and Lina Stierenburg, both of Golden, were
  licensed to wed.
FINK, Miss Gussie   Augusta   Jun 14, 1900
  Married this Wednesday eve at the home of A.M. Working, Miss Gussie Fink to
  Fred Johnson, of St Marys by Rev Ferguson. Bride has resided with Workings
  the past ten years. Groom is son of Hiram Johnson who is a prosperous farmer
  of St Marys. Will live with grooms parents.

Page 26

FINLEY, F.S.   Big Neck   Feb 14, 1901
    F.S. Finley and wife attended the marriage of Mrs Finley's sister near
    Columbus Thursday.
FLEMING, Enoch   Oct 14, 1904
    See Dunlap, Miss Mabel
FLEMING, George   York Neck   Apr 27, 1899
    Married, George Fleming and Mrs Nancy Pierce. Will live in the home of the
    groom in lower York Neck. Married Tuesday night a low twelve.
FLEMING, Mr and Mrs George   York Neck   May 4, 1899
    Supplement Mr and Mrs George Fleming's union was of short duration, as
    they parted last Friday evening. Cause is unknown.
FLESNER, Albert   Local   Feb 26, 1904
    A marriage license issued Friday to Albert Flesner, of Clayton and Miss
    Ricke Post, of the same village.
FLESNER, Albert   Local   Feb 26, 1904
    Albert Flesner and Miss Rieka Post were married Sunday at the Prairie
    Church by Rev Oetting. Groom is son of H.J. Flesner and bride is daughter
    of Gerd Post.
FLESNER, Ekke   Local   Mar 25, 1904
    Ekke Flesner and Miss Margaret Ideus, of this village were married Monday
    eve at East Side Church by Rev Dorrow. Will live in Golden in the property
    owned by the groom and now occupied by Louie Trescher.
FLESNER, Gerhard W.   Married   Mar 10, 1905
    Mr Gerhard W. Flesner and Miss Minnie Eber, of LaPrairie were married at
    their home in Golden Sunday March 5 at 2 PM by Rev Alpers. Dinner was
    served at 3. Groom is son of W.H. Flesner.Sr., formerly of South Prairie
    and has been for some time in employ, F.M. King, of Augusta, at his store
    in Golden. Bride is daughter of Henry Eber, of LaPrairie. Will live in
    their nicely furnished home on N. Congress St. which Gerhard has provided.
FLESNER, Mary   Mar 18, 1893   Apr 18, 1901
    See Carstins, Dick
FLESNER, Simon W.   Wedding   Oct 14, 1904
    Simon W. Flesner and Miss Maggie Bruns were married at the South Prairie
    Church Sunday 11 AM by Rev Oetting. Bride attended by Misses Anna Bruns
    and Minnie Eber. Groom by Fred Bruns and George Flesner. Groom is son of
    Wm H. Flesner Sr and a brother of George Flesner the clothing man of Golden
    Bride is daughter of John Bruns of South Prairie. Reception at brides home
    Sunday for near relatives. Will live on the Wm Flesner Sr farm, east of
    Golden.
FLESNER, Miss Tina   Feb 15, 1902
    See Weert, Eilert Jr.
FLESSNER, Antje   Jul 31, 1897
    See Franzen, Hinrich
FLESSNER, Gerd H.   February 1893   Feb 21, 1901
    February 18--Gerd H. Flessner and Miss Hirska Weerts were licensed to be we
FLESSNER, Miss Helena   Jan 16, 1897
    See Fritzen, Martin
FLESSNER, W.H.   Local   Mar 14, 1896
    Married, Friday eve, March 6th, at the Prairie German Church, W.H. Flessner
    and Miss Anna Eggan, of Clayton township by Rev Oetting.
FLETCHER, Fred   Camp Point   Apr 10, 1897
    Fred Fletcher and Miss Dollie Welch were married at the home of the bride
    Sunday at 4 PM.
FOLKERS, Miss Etta   Feb 6, 1902
    See Bauer, William

FOLLUM, Miss Eva A.   Oct 2, 1903
    See Adair, Curtis
FORD, Ed   March 1894   Mar 30, 1899
    Ed Ford and Miss Rosa Kimball, were married in this city by Squire Duis.
FORD, Ed   Review   Jun 12, 1902
    March 31, 1894   Ed Ford and Miss Rosa Kimball were married.
FOREST, Miss Maggie   Coatsburg   Dec 24, 1896
    Miss Maggie Forest, age 14 years was married at Quincy Friday to John Leoffel,
    age 28. They applied for license day before and were refused, but re-
    turned Friday with the girls guardian and procured it. It's a hard
    blow Henry.
FORSEY, Miss Sadie   Nov 18, 1904
    See Randall, Lewis
FOWLER, Eva   May 6, 1898
    See Peil, Henry
FRANCIS, Mrs Margaret   Camp Point   Mar 16, 1899
    On April 3rd at high noon at the home of Mr and Mrs Samuel Francis will
    occur the wedding of Mr Housler and Mrs Margaret Francis, of Quincy.
    Will live Galesburg. Mr Housler is a mail clerk and Mrs Francis is a
    former Camp Point lady.
FRANKEN, Miss Christina   Locals   Feb 24, 1905
    Miss Christina Franken, of Chicago, came Thursday to attend the wedding
    of her mother.
FRANKEN, Mrs Engeline   Feb 24, 1905
    See Leenerts, Leenert
FRANKEN, Geska G.   May 17, 1900
    See Freirichs, Mensse H.
FRANKS, Miss Nonae   Exchange   Sep 8, 1905
    Miss Nonae Franks, of Clayton was married to Wm C. Bradley at Quincy Tuesday.
FRANZEN, Anna C.   8 Years Ago   Jul 4, 1901
    See Detmers, Christopher H.
FRANZEN, Miss Catherine   Aug 28, 1903
    See Cassens, George
FRANZEN, Cobus   Local   Sep 2, 1904
    News from Idaho says that our neighbor, Cobus Franzen, who went west for
    his health, was recently married to Mrs Tretie Peil formerly of this place.
FRANZEN, Fred   5 Years Ago   Jan 22, 1898
    Fred Franzen and Miss Annie Buss were married at the home of R.A. Buss.
FRANZEN, Fred B.   January 1893   Jan 10, 1901
    January 14--Fred B. Franzen and Miss Anna Buss were married.
FRANZEN, Hinrich   Golden Wedding   Jul 31. 1897
    Fifty years ago in Germany occurred the marriage of Hinrich Franzen and
    Antje Flessner of this neighborhood, about 200 of our citizens, mostly
    relatives helped celebrate. During the afternoon, according to an old
    German custom, a collection must be taken up for some worthy cause, and
    Harm H. Franzen was instructed to collect what money he could to assist
    a student who the church is trying to help. John Franzen enlivened the
    occasion by several comic songs. Harm Franzens children and others rendered
    vocal selections. Mr and Mrs Franzen have lived this locality since
    January 1850 and with one exception are the oldest German residents. All
    the children were present with exception of two, who live in Nebraska.
    (This is a very long write up and you'll have to get a copy.)
FRANZEN, Miss Lena   Feb 8, 1900
    See Piel, Fred

FRANZEN, Miss Mary   Jan 29, 1904
    See Arbogast, Clayton
FRANZEN, Miss Tena   Sep 18, 1902
    See Miller, Claus
FRAZER, Miss Ada   Local   Jul 1, 1898
    Invitations are out for marriage of Miss Ada Frazer to Mr John M. Wallace
    at the home of Mrs Emma Frazer on Wednesday eve July 6th.
FRAZIER, Miss Ada   Local   Jul 8, 1898
    Miss Ada Frazier and John Wallace were married at the home of the brides
    mother in this city Wednesday eve by Rev M.W. Lorimer, pastor of the United
    Presbyterian Church. Mr Wallace is associated with Heimburger Bros. in
    the marble and granite business.
FREDERICK, Miss Alice   Oct 9, 1903
    See Beer, Irwin
FREDERICK, Miss Anna   Aug 22, 1901
    See Miller, George
FREDERICKS, Chris   Double Wedding   Mar 27, 1897
    Sunday occurred the marriage of four of Goldens young people, Chris
    Fredericks and Miss Mary Ehnen and Aime Ehnen and Miss Hannah Weyen at
    the East Side Lutheran Church by Rev Dorrow.
FREDERICKS, Martin   Mar 24, 1905
    See Buss, Miss Emma
FREIRICHS, Mensse H.   Local   May 17, 1900
    At the Prairie Lutheran Church yesterday at 3 PM, Mensse H. Freirichs, of
    Peoria and Geska G. Franken, of Golden were married by Rev Oetting.
    Reception at Franken residence. Will live Chicago.
FRENCH, Rev   Aug 21, 1903
    See Worman, Miss Nellie
FRIDAY, Charlie F.   Jun 12, 1897
    See Logsdon, Lillie
FRIEDRICKS, Christian   Local   May 17, 1900
    Christian Friedricks and Mrs Ricka Huisman were married at the home of the
    groom two miles west of Golden last Sunday afternoon by Rev Dorow.
FRITZEN, George   Feb 16, 1899
    See Buss, Miss Katie
FRITZEN, Martin   Married   Jan 16, 1897
    Sunday afternoon occurred the marriage of two Prairie young people, Martin
    Fritzen and Miss Helena Flessner, daughter of John Flessner and wife by
    Rev Oetting, pastor of the Prairie Church. Mr Fritzen returned from
    Nebraska last week where he spent the past year. Will live with Mr and
    Mrs Flessner as Helena is youngest daughter and all the daughter at home.
FRUEHLING, Miss Julia   Apr 18, 1901
    See Buss, John W.
FRUHLING, Minka   Married   Feb 17, 1905
    Minka Fruhling, of Raymond, Minnesota has been visiting relatives in this
    vicinity two months. True light of his visit came to light when he mar-
    ried Miss Jennie Goudschal, daughter of Mr and Mrs Ed Goudschal of
    LaPrairie. They were married at Salem Church at Quincy, Wednesday, by
    Rev Kramer of that Church. Will move to a farm near Raymond, Minnesota
    after a few weeks where Mr Fruhling is comfortably situated.
FRUKEN, Anna   Sep 9, 1904
    See Lehroff, Hye
FUHR, Mr Edward Wilson   Jun 24, 1904
    See Beckett, Miss Bessie

FUNK, Florence Pearl   Local   Apr 21, 1905
    Cards are out by Mr and Mrs James E. Funk, residing East of town to witness
    the marriage of their daughter, Florence Pearl, to Albert C. Luckel,
    Thursday April 20 at 7. "Camp Point Journal"
    Mr Luckel is coming to Golden to start a blacksmith shop. He has his
    building completed and his supplies arrived Wednesday. They will no
    doubt move to Golden in the near future.

FURGERSON, Charles   Neighborhood   Mar 20, 1897
    Wedding at Naples last Sunday eve, Charles Furgerson and Mrs Susan Neal.
    Groom is 21 years old and bride is 42 years old. Marriage made the young
    man a step grandpa.

GANS, Miss Mattie E.   Nov 21, 1901
    See Thomas, Joseph L.

GANS, Miss Maud   Jun 14, 1900
    See Pierce, Samuel

GANZ, Miss Jessie   Dec 4, 1897
    See Klepper, Clyde E.

GARARD, Miss Kate   Mar 21, 1901
    See Hatfield, George

GARNER, Perlia   Mar 13, 1902
    See Carlin, Wm F.

GARNER, Sela   March 3, 1894   Jun 12, 1902
    See Miller, Wm

GARRELTS, John: Mar 16, 1898
    See Saathoff, Miss Antke

GARRETT, Miss Grace   Camp Point   May 30, 1901
    June 5th, at the home of Mr and Mrs John Garrett will occur the wedding
    of their daughters, Miss Grace to Orval Hunsaker and Miss Jennie to
    Ernest Wisehart.

GARRETT, Miss Jennie   Camp Point   May 30, 1901
    See Garrett, Miss Grace (sisters double wedding)

GARRETT, Miss Olive   May 27, 1904
    See Pittman, James H.

GARRETT, Peter   Camp Point   Jun 12, 1903
    Peter Garrett and Gertrude Oliver were married at the home of Miss Oliver
    Wednesday eve of last week.

GARRETTS, John   Mar 16, 1898
    See Saathoff, Miss Antka

GATES, Oliver   Local   May 1, 1903
    Oliver Gates, of Columbus, and Miss Stella Suter, of Houston, were married
    April 19, at the Methodist parsonage in Camp Point. They will live on
    Sam Simmonds farm in Columbus township.

GAY, Charles V.   Local   Apr 14, 1905
    Charles V. Gay, of Camp Point, president of the Camp Point Bank and Mrs
    Annie F. Kelley, also of Camp Point, were married Sunday at 6 AM by
    Rev W.T. Reynolds, pastor of the Presbyterian Church and left that AM
    for Chicago to spend their honeymoon.

GEIBERT,   Horeb   Feb 13, 1897
    Frank Heubner and daughter, Miss Lena, attended the Geibert wedding in
    Quincy last Wednesday.

GEIBERT, Mrs D.E.   Dec 30, 1904
    See Asher, Warren

GEIBERT, John   From old New Era's   Sep 18, 1902
    October 6, 1894 John Geibert and Miss Etta Turner were married.

GERDES, George E.   Local   Mar 11, 1904
    Marriage license issued Wednesday to George E. Gerdes, of Bowen, and Miss
    Hattie Gronewold, of LaPrairie.
GERJETS, John B.   5 Years Ago   Feb 13, 1897
    See Adams, Miss Hattie B.
GERJETS, John D.   Local   Jul 26, 1900
    John D. Gerjets and Miss Fredericka Behrens were married at the Prairie
    Church last Thursday eve by Rev Oetting.
GERJETS, Tina   Nov 2, 1899
    See Lubben, John H.
GETTS, Charlie   Camp Point   May 1, 1897
    Married since our last letterm Charlie Getts and Sadie Caldwell at Christia
    parsonage by Elder O. Dilley.
GIBBS, Miss Clara   Nov 20, 1903
    See Shake, William J.
GIBNEY, Michael   Big Neck   Nov 2, 1899
    Last Wednesday Michael Gibney and his housekeeper, Mrs Courtney, were made
    man and wife by a priest in Mendon.
GIBSON, Joseph H.   Houston   Oct 16, 1897
    Joseph H. Gibson, of this place and Miss Matilda Laird, of Mt Vernon, Ill.
    were married Sunday October 3rd, at the home of the brides parents, Mr and
    Mrs David Laird, by Rev. J.C. Kinison, pastor in charge of Mt Vernon ME
    Church.
GIBSON, Joseph H.   Married   Oct 16, 1897
    Married at Mt Vernon, Illinois October 3rd, Joseph H. Gibson of Chatten and
    Miss Matilda Laird of Mt Vernon. Groom is son of James Gibson of Keene
    township and bride a number of years ago was resident of same neighborhood,
    Will live Houston. "Camp Point Journal"
GIBSON, Miss Nellie   Clayton   Jan 5, 1899
    Married at the Hampton House at 3 PM Wednesday, Mr Henry L. Reed and Miss
    Nellie Gibson, the young lady who has lived in McDowells family several
    months by Rev P. Slagle, pastor of Methodist Church of which they are
    members.
GIBSON, Miss Winnie   Texas   Jan 16, 1902
    Anderson Hatton and Miss Winnie Gibson, who were married last week are
    stopping at present with Pa Hatton.
GILBERT, Miss Louisa M.   Feb 12, 1904
    See Leach, Francis L.
GILLEPSIE, Henry S.   Local   Dec 26, 1901
    Henry S. Gillepsie, of Huntsville, and Miss Hannah Schwanke, of LaPrairie,
    were licensed to marry Tuesday.
GLAZE, W.W.   Apr 11, 1896
    See Tyler, Miss Myrtie
GOLDENSTEIN, Mrs Lena   Mar 13, 1903
    See Busboom, Heye T.
GOLDENSTEIN, Oltman W.   Married in Honey Creek   Mar 20, 1903
    Married, Wednesday March 11th at 1:30 PM at the home of the brides mother,
    Mrs R.W. Ewen, Mr Oltman W. Goldenstein, of Golden to Miss Lizzie M. Ewen,
    of Mendon by Rev Drexel, pastor of the Lutheran Church at Coatsburg. Bride
    is second daughter of Mrs R.W. Ewen. Groom is son of Wm. Goldenstein,
    who died some years ago, leaving him a prosperous farmer. Will live with
    groom's mother.
GOLDENSTEIN, Oltman W.   Local   Mar 13, 1903
    Oltman W. Goldenstein, and Lizzie Ewen, of Mendon were married last week an
    will live on the Goldenstein place in Clayton township.

GOODING, Miss Eliza   Jan 2, 1902
   See Rulifson, Claude
GOODING, Miss Eliza   Chatten   Jan 9, 1902
   Mr C. Rufleson, a prominent farmer of Iowa, and Miss Eliza Gooding, of this
   place were married January 1st at the home of the brides parents, by Rev
   Wehrman. Left for their new home that evening.
GOODING, Miss Sarah   Nov 13, 1897
   See Junk, Edwin
GOODNOW, Fred H.   Nov 6, 1903
   Fred H. Goodnow of Loraine and Miss Sadie L. Smith, of the same place,
   were licensed to wed Wednesday.
GOOSMAN, John R.   Local   Oct 16, 1903
   At the home of brides mother in this village, Wednesday eve at 8, John R.
   Goosman and Miss Mary Janssen were married. Will take a wedding trip to
   Nebraska.
GOUDSCHAL, Gottlieb   Local   Feb 13, 1903
   At the East Side Church last Sunday Gottlieb Goudschal and Miss Lena Leenerts,
   of LaPrairie were married.
GOUDSCHAL, Miss Jennie   Feb 17, 1905
   See Fruhling, Minka
GOUDSHALL, Gottlieb   Local   Feb 6, 1903
   Marriage license issued Tuesday to Gottlieb Goudshall and Lena Leenerts,
   of LaPrairie.
GRAGG, Oscar   Jun 24, 1898
   See Eells, Miss Grace
GRAGG, Oscar O.   Augusta   Jun 24, 1898
   Married Wednesday eve June 15th Oscar O. Gragg, the Boston Clothing Store's
   genial clerk and Miss Grace Eells of Bowen. Will live Augusta.
GRAHAM, Miss Grace   Oct 6, 1905
   See Strickler, Joe
GRAHAM, Grace   Wedding   Oct 13, 1905
   Wednesday eve October 4th at home of brides parents, Mr and Mrs Sanford
   Graham occurred the marriage of their daughter, Grace, to Mr Joseph Strickler
   of Loraine by Rev W.A. Taylor. Miss Nellie Strickler played the wedding
   march. Groom is a young farmer and takes his bride to a home fitted in
   cozy style for a king and queen. Attending from a far was: Mr and Mrs
   E.C. Swaney, of Chicago, Mr and Mrs Luther Eckles, of Graham, Missouri,
   Mr and Mrs Sam Eckles of Graham, Missouri. On Thursday Mr and Mrs W.
   Strickler tendered the bridal couple an infare at which 50 guests were
   present.
GREENBACK, Mrs Tat   Round about us   Jan 18, 1896
   Mrs Tat Greenback of Colchester has eloped with one Harvey Russell, and
   gone to parts unknown. She made an even divide of the children, taking
   one along and leaving one with its father.
GRIGGS, Geo.   Augusta   Jun 24, 1898
   Married Wednesday eve June 15th Geo. Griggs of Bowen and Miss Ora Irwin of
   Bowen. Will live in Adrian where he has a position in a store.
GRIGGS, George   Jun 24, 1898
   See Irwin, Miss Ora M.
GRIGSON, Fred R.   Camp Point   Dec 18, 1897
   Fred R. Grigson and Miss Flora Willis were married December 7th in Augusta
   at the home of Elder Carpenter.
GRIGSON, Fred R.   Camp Point   Dec 18, 1897
   Fred R. Grigson and Miss Flora Willis were married Dec 7th in Augusta at the
   home of Elder Carpenter. Mr Grigson has many friends here and in Golden.

GRIMES. Dr J.M.   Camp Point   Nov 17, 1898
    Married, Dr J.M. Grimes and Miss Lizzie E. Taylor by Rev T.M. Dillen at
    7 PM. last Thursday at the home of the groom.
GRONEWOLD, Miss Anna   Local   Feb 24, 1905
    Miss Anna Gronewold, daughter of Wm Gronewold, and Mr Geo. Johnson, of
    Peoria will be married at Trinity Lutheran Church in Golden Sunday eve
    February 26th. Will live 309 Goodwin Ave. Peoria after March 10th.
GRONEWOLD, Miss Anna   Mar 3, 1905
    See Johnson, Geo.
GRONEWOLD, Miss Hattie   Mar 11, 1904
    See Gerdes, George E.
GRONEWOLD, Ida J.   Feb 10, 1905
    See Schone, George J.
GRONEWOLD, William   Local   Mar 11, 1904
    William Gronewold and Miss Helkea Leenerts, of this village were married at
    the East Side Church by Rev Dorrow Saturday at 7 PM. Groom is son of Wm
    Gronewold Sr. and bride is daughter of Oltman Leenerts.
GRONEWOLD, William   Local   Nov 18, 1904
    Marriage of William Gronewold to Miss Margaret Eigenberg is announced as of
    Thursday November 24th. Mr Gronewold is son of Men Gronewold, of near
    Chatten and Miss Eigenberg is daughter of Mr and Mrs John Eigenberg of near
    Golden. Will live on the Eigenberg farm moving then about December 10th.
GRONEWOLD, William   Local   Dec 2, 1904
    Thursday at 8 PM of last week at the home of brides parents occurred the
    marriage of Mr William Gronewold to Margaret Eigenberg little Luellen
    Jansen, age 3 years was flower girl and played the part of an attendant
    with perfect ease. Rev J.H. Utesch, of Liberty performed the ceremony.
    On Friday Mr and Mrs Gronewold drove to Liberty, returning Sunday night.
GROSE, Henry K.   Local   Jan 29, 1904
    On Monday eve at Camp Point, Henry K. Grose and Miss Gertrude Allen of that
    village were married. Mr Grose is an evangelistic singer, and assisted in
    the tent meeting at Camp Point last summer.
GROSS, Miss Tillie   Apr 11, 1896
    See Hopka, Henry
GROVES, Daniel R.   Local   Aug 24, 1899
    Daniel R. Groves and Miss Jennie Shrader, both of Big Neck, were married at
    Methodist parsonage in Camp Point last Thursday by Rev T.M. Dillon.
    Mr Groves is a member of the firm Groves Bros. of Big Neck.
GROVES, Freeman   Local   Oct 2, 1903
    Freeman Groves and Miss Cornelia Rice, both of Plymouth, were married at
    Quincy, Sunday.
GROVES, Miss Lula   Dec 21, 1899
    See Bacon, Wm Jr
GROVES, Miss Maude M.   Apr 5, 1900
    See Schroeder, Paul
GRUBB, Miss Ella M.   Jul 10, 1902
    See Simmons, Jas. W.
GRUNY, Geo.   8 Years Ago   Dec 12, 1901
    September 9, 1893 Geo. Gruny and Miss Anna Asher, of Camp Point, were
    married.
GUENTHER, Miss Lena Kate   Married   Dec 1, 1905
    On Sunday 6 PM November 26th at home of brides parents occurred the marriag
    of Miss Lena Kate, daughter of Mr and Mrs Louis Guenther, to Mr John M.L.
    Schroeder by Rev Shruge, pastor of Lutherna Church at Coatsburg. Bride is
    second daughter of Mr and Mrs Guenther. Groom is fifth son of Mr and Mrs

L.C. Schroeder. Messrs Albert Schroeder and Willie Murrah acted as grrooms-
man and Misses Cora Guenther and Sophia Schroeder acted as bridesmaids.
HACKNEY, Miss Hila   Mar 27, 1903
   See Gordon, Samuel
HACKNEY, Mrs Millie   Dec 26, 1901
   See Hollis, J.C.
HACKNEY, Miss Nora   Local   Feb 19, 1904
   A marriage license was issued Saturday to Elzie Richardson, of Lebanon,
   Virginia and Miss Nora Hackney, of Golden.
HACKNEY, Miss Nora   Elm Grove   Feb 19, 1904
   Miss Nora Hackney and Mr Elza Richardson, lately of Lebanon, Russell County
   Virginia went before Justice John Alexander last Sunday afternoon and were
   married. Will live on a farm rented by Henry Dutton. Bride is daughter
   of Mr and Mrs Samuel Hackney, now residents of Texas.
HACKNEY, Wm D.   Historical   Apr 18, 1901
   March 18, 1893 Wm D. Hackney and Mary B. Hughes were licensed to wed.
HAGY, Miss Ada   Feb 15, 1902
   See Alexander, Sid
HAIL, Mr   Camp Point   Dec 26, 1896
   Mr Hail and Miss Lillie Suddett, of near Denver, will be married at the
   bride's home on Christmas eve. Miss Suddett is well known here and in
   Golden.
HAINES, James   Loraine Elopement   Apr 24, 1897
   Reported from Loraine, an uncle running away with his 16 year old niece.
   On Sunday James Haines went to church with little Lizzie Hudson, the
   daughter of his sister and after church the two were seen walking in
   opposite direction of girls home. Both are missing. Yesterday Wren
   Hudson, father of the girl swore out warrent for James arrest. It is
   thought they went to St Louis or Iowa where girl has relatives. "Whig"
   FOR CORRECTION SEE Hynes, Wakeman.
HAISTINGS, Miss Edna   May 1, 1902
   See Shay, James
HAMILTON, Mrs Mila   Elm Grove   Aug 28, 1897
   Mrs Mila Hamilton, of Cisco, Piatt County is among early life friends,
   visiting. She will be remembered as Miss Mila Hinson, afterwards Mrs
   Lewis Cain, after the death of Mr Cain in Piatt County she married again.
   Her present name is Hamilton.
HANKE, John   Clayton   Jan 5, 1899
   A wedding at German Lutheran Church in Concord township Wednesday eve.
   John Hanke, youngest son of Mr Fred Hanke and Miss Emma Vollbracht,
   daughter of Mr and Mrs William Vollbracht of Concord by Rev George
   Blicvernicht.
HARBERTS, Jurgen H.   Married   Jan 11, 1900
   Wednesday, of last week, Jurgen H. Harberts and Miss Minnie Eigenburg,
   both of Golden, went to Quincy and that evening were married by a Lutheran
   minister at his residence at 9th and State Streets. Bride is daughter of
   John Eigenburg of this village. Have gone to housekeeping at their home
   in the north part of town.
HARBERTS, Miss Katie   January 1893   Jan 17, 1901
   See Weyen, John
HARBERTS, Miss Kate   Jan 22, 1898
   See Weyen, John

HARBERTS, Miss Ollie   Local   Jun 19, 1897
 Married at the family residence in this city Thursday afternoon at 3,
 Miss Ollie Harberts to Mr Frank Meyer, of La Prairie by Rev Darrow of the
 East Side German Church. Mr Meyre has been in the vicinity two or three
 years. Will live on a farm between Chatten and Bowen.
HARBOR, J.F.   Feb 27, 1897
 See Jurgens, Miss Annie
HARDING, Ernest   Clayton   Oct 13, 1898
 Marriage of Mr Ernest Harding and Miss Allyen Norris a lady of Mt Sterling
 will be Sunday the 16th inst at Quincy.
HARRAH, Miss Jessie   Feb 10, 1905
 See Vertrees, Ray
HARRIS, Eva Pearl   Sep 27, 1900
 See McGill, Sydney A.
HARRIS, Miss Lula   Feb 22, 1900
 See Klem, Will
HARRIS, Margaret   Dec 12, 1902
 See Hedrick, Willis
HART, Ben   Camp Point   Apr 24, 1902
 Ben Hart and a young lady of Altoona, Illinois were married Sunday.
HARTLEY, Rev D.H.   Married   Feb 5, 1904
 Thursday at 4 PM in ME Church of Elvston, Rev D.H. Hartley and Miss Lottie
 Salome Ruddell were married by Rev J.E. Mercer, the brides pastor. They
 left for Golden after ceremony and receive callers after February 15th.
 Rev Hartley is a native of Virginia and graduate of Illinois Wesleyan
 University and now serving Golden ME Church. Brides parents live on a
 farm near Elvaston and is a graduate of the Wesleyan College of Music at
 Bloomington, Illinois and has been teaching music.
HARTLY, Herbet   La Prairie   Apr 29, 1898
 Herbet Hartly and Bertha Young were married last eve at the parsonage by
 Rev Douglas. Missy was a former resident of LaPrairie.
HASCHEMEYER, Miss Mary   Jan 1, 1904
 See Buhr, Fred
HASHAMYER, Edward   Local   Feb 15, 1902
 Two prominent young people of the vicinity east of Golden were married at
 Prairie Church after the morning service Sunday. They were Edward Hashamye
 a son of Chris Hashamyer and Miss Hattie Bruns, a daughter of John Bruns.
 Henry Bruns acted as groomsman and Miss Mary Hashamyer as bridesmaid. Next
 week they will move to Minnesota where Mr Hashamyer will engage in farming.
HATCHER, Mrs Helen   Round About Us   Jan 25, 1896
 Pittsfield Democrat Mrs Helen Hatcher, whose late husband, John R. Hatcher
 shot himself while a divorce suit brought by her was pending, and died
 shortly after it was granted was married here Monday to David Young, of
 Pearl. This is her fifth marriage.
HATFIELD, George   Chili   Mar 21, 1901
 George Hatfield, of Chili and Miss Kate Garard of Braddock, Pennsylvania
 were married at Carthage last Wednesday, March 13th.
HATTON, Anderson   Jan 16, 1902
 See Gibson, Miss Winnie
HATTON, Anderson   Local   Jan 16, 1902
 Anderson L. Hatton, of Loraine, and Miss Winifred Gibson of the same neigh-
 borhood, were married last week.
HAWLEY, Miss Nettie   Augusta   May 31, 1900
 Miss Nettie Hawley, formerly of this place, but now of Galesburg, was re-
 cently married to H.C. Johnson.

HAZLETT, Mrs Etta   Oct 2, 1903
    See Clark, Frank
HEDRICK, Miss Alice   Oct 30, 1903
    See Manlove, Roy
HEDRICK, Dr E.G.   From old New Era's   Jul 24, 1902
    June 16, 1894 Cards are out announcing the wedding of Dr E.G. Hedrick and
    Miss Margaret James.
HEDRICK, Miss Effie   Sep 25, 1897
    See Stanley, Wm
HEDRICK, Miss Mabel   Local   Dec 27, 1900
    Dr Hedrick and family, Albert Hedrick and sister, Miss Grace, went to Loraine
    Tuesday to attend the wedding of their niece, Miss Mabel Hedrick, to Rev
    Claude Haskill of Canton, Missouri.
HEDRICK, Miss Pearl   Jan 16, 1903
    See Walker, Chas.
HEDRICK, Willis   Local   Dec 12, 1902
    Marriage license was issued this week to Willis Hedrick, of Loraine, and
    Margaret Harris, of Macomb.
HEINECKE, Miss Anna   Oct 16, 1903
    See Bruns, Henry
HEINECKE, Charles   Local   Dec 26, 1901
    Charles Heinecke, of LaPrairie and Miss Laura E. Johnson, nurse at Woodland
    Home, were married at Carthage last week by Rev Ayleng of the ME Church.
    Will live at LaPrairie.
HENDRICKS, Eilt   Jan 29, 1899
    See Buss, Miss Jennie
HENDRICKS, Miss Jennie   Mar 27, 1902
    See Castle, Richard
HENDRICKS, Miss Jessie   Apr 3, 1902
    See Castle, Richard
HENNING, George   Local   Feb 5, 1904
    A marriage license was issued Wednesday to George Henning and Miss Rose
    Martin of Camp Point.
HENRY, Mrs C.E.   Local   Jan 8, 1898
    Dr S. Henry received telegram from Omaha Tuesday PM telling of daughter in
    law, Mrs C.E. Henry, after illness of two weeks. Mrs Henry was married
    last August in Chicago to Dr Ed C. Henry and went with him to Omaha where
    he is professor in a medical school. She was Miss Edith J. Stahl, daughter
    of Mr and Mrs Elias Stahl, of Camp Point. Funeral at Presbyterian Church
    at 2:30 PM Thursday.   Camp Point Journal
HENRY, Dr E.C.   Camp Point   Aug 28, 1897
    Dr E.C. Henry left Monday for Chicago where he will be married to Miss Edith
    Stahl of that city. Will live Omaha, Nebraska.
HENRY, Miss Fannie   Sep 21, 1899
    See Bates, Dr Lee
HENRY, Hez   Camp Point   May 1, 1897
    Hez Henry and Mattie Farlow were married in Quincy last Wednesday eve.
HENRY, Hez G.   Local   Apr 24, 1897
    Hez G. Henry, cashier of the People's Bank at Camp Point and Miss Mattie
    Farlow, assistant cashier were married at Quincy Thursday.
HERREN, Miss Kate   Oct 21, 1904
    See Paben, Henry
HERRING, Miss Edith   Big Neck   Jan 24, 1901
    Promptly at 6 PM January 16th at the home of brides mother, in Big Neck,
    in presence of relatives and friends, Miss Edith Herring and C.E. Beer, of
    Clayton, were married by Rev F.P. Bonnefon.

HERRON, Henry   Local   Apr 17, 1897
  Henry Herron and Miss Annie Ehnen were married in East Side German Church
  Saturday 4 PM by Rev Darrow.
HESLER, Charles   York Neck   Nov 27, 1897
  Sunday at 1 PM occured the marriage of Charles Hesler and Ollie Reed.
HESTER, Eliza   Dec 26, 1901
  See Hester, Wm
HESTER, Wm   Houston   Dec 26, 1901
  Weddings of Wm Hester and Iva Louderback and Wm Webster and Eliza Hester
  will take place some time this week.
HEUBNER, Miss Lena   Elm Grove   Jan 8, 1898
  Miss Lena Heubner and Charles Marsh will be married at the home of Frank
  Heubner next Sunday.
HIGHTOWER, Miss Carrie   Jun 24, 1904
  See Anderson, Herma L.
HILLYER, Warren   Local   Apr 20, 1899
  Marriage license issued at Quincy to Warren Hillyer of Huntsville and Miss
  Orpha Cain of near Augusta.
HILLYER, Dr Warren E.   Apr 27, 1899
  See Cain, Orpha M.
HIMILTON, Miss   Dec 2, 1897
  See Williams, Wilbur L.
HINTZ, Wm and Minnie   Miserable Married Men   Jul 4, 1896
  Divorce decree signed Wm Hintz vs Minnie Hintz
HIRONS, Miss Sadie   Jan 4, 1900
  See Campbell, Charles O.
HIRONS, Wm   January 1893   Jan 17, 1901
  January 21 Wm Hirons and Miss Jennie E. Acklem were married at Camp Poin
HOBBS, Miss Lulu   Aug 7, 1903
  See Syckle, George E.
HOCAMP, Miss Lizzie   Jan 22, 1898
  See Sharp, Amos
HOCAMP, Miss Mary   Dec 28, 1899
  See Buetel, Frank
HOCH, Ed   Jun 28, 1900
  See Dorsey, Pearl
HODGSON, Miss   Jun 20, 1901
  See Baldwin, John
HODGSON, Miss Mabel   Oct 20, 1905
  See Bottorff, Harry
HOEVELER, Miss Katerine   Sep 22, 1898
  See Argast, Will
HOKE, Mr and Mrs Craven   Camp Point   Nov 13, 1897
  Mr and Mrs Craven Hoke, of Kirksville, Missouri celebrated their 15th
  wedding anniversary Thursday.
HOKE, John H.   Local   Dec 5, 1902
  John H. Hoke, of Camp Point and Miss Nettie Jewett, of Clayton, were mar-
  ried last week.
HOLLIS, J.C.   Local   Dec 26, 1901
  J.C. Hollis, of Galesburg, and Mrs Millie Hackney, of this village, were
  married in Chicago Monday. Groom is a successful traveling salesman.
HONNOLD, Miss Margaret   Local   Dec 1, 1905
  Miss Margaret Honnold, of Camp Point, and Mr Dick Rhea were married at
  Caney, Kansas Monday. Their marriage was a surprise ro their friends.

HOPKA, Henry   Elm Grove   Apr 11, 1896
  Henry Hopka and Miss Tillie Gross, of Pea Ridge township Brown County were
  married at the home of brides father last Wednesday at high noon by Rev Bell
  pastor of the C.P. Soci-- Horeb Church. Reception at home of grooms
  parents, Mr and Mrs Fred Hopka Thursday eve.
HOPPER, Miss Rena Mae   Oct 2, 1903
  See Cain, Clarence
HORNECKER, Edwin   Camp Point   Jan 22, 1898
  Edwin Hornecker and Miss Lulu Allen were married last Wednesday.
HORNER, Miss Nellie   Mar 19, 1898
  See Meyers, Henry
HORNEY, Arthur   Dec 18, 1903
  See Black, Ethel
HORNEY, Earl   Local   Jan 26, 1899
  Earl Horney of Bowen and Miss Daisy Bennet of near Chatten, were married at
  the home of brides parents last Thursday at noon by Rev Wehrman, of this city.
HOSKINS, Erastus   Local   Jan 23, 1902
  Erastus Hoskins and Mrs Malinda Reeves, of Coatsburg, were married last week.
HOSTETTER, Alvin   Camp Point   Dec 7, 1899
  Alvin Hostetter and Miss Pearl Cannon were married in Jacksonville last
  Thursday. Mr Hostetter is a carpenter and is working at his trade. Bride
  will return here and finish her school east of town.
HOSTETTER, Clarence   Local   Mar 20, 1903
  Clarence Hostetter and Miss Carrie Craver, of Camp Point were married at
  Galesburg, Tuesday.
HOSTETTER, Miss Cornie   Sep 25, 1903
  See Clark, Jesse
HOSTETTER, Julian C.   Local   Sep 11, 1903
  Julian C. Hostetter and Miss Myrtle E. Omer, of Camp Point, were married
  last week.
HOUCK, Miss Lizzie   Feb 17, 1905
  See Stover, Frederick
HOUSE, Miss Mary   Feb 22, 1896
  See Bell, John
HOUSLER, Mr   Mar 16, 1899
  See Francis, Mrs Margaret
HOWE, Miss   Apr 20, 1899
  See Coleman, Gabe
HOWLAND, Miss Hattie   Local   Oct 23, 1897
  Miss Hattie Howland well known in this place was married at Galesburg
  this week.
HOYT, B.F.   8 Years Ago   Dec 12, 1901
  September 23, 1893   B.F. Hoyt and Miss Jennie Bottorff were married.
HOYT, W.R.   Local   Jan 15, 1898
  W.R. Hoyt, of North East township, is justly entitled to be called an old
  settler. He has lived in North East township since 1843. Married in 1852
  and lived here since on the same farm. He was 68 years old on the 8th
  inst and might have been named Andrew Jackson if his father had been a
  democrat.   Camp Point Journal
HOYT, Mr and Mrs W.R.   Golden Wedding   Feb 20, 1902
  (Special to Quincy Whig) Augusta, Ill February 17 Celebration of golden
  wedding of Mr and Mrs W.R. Hoyt, residents of North East township Adams
  County Ill at their home five miles southeast of Augusta. About 60 relatives and friends met at the beautiful home at 10 o'clock and spent the
  day. From a distance were: Mrs Ned James of Beardstown, Mr and Mrs '

Charles Brooking and family, from Macomb, Mr Chas. Hoyt, from Golden,
Mrs Anna Crain, of Washington D.C. besides many friends from Augusta
and vicinity.

HUCKLEBURY, Miss Stella   Apr 24, 1897
  See Selby, Elmer T.

HUDSON, Miss Anna   Mar 16, 1899
  See Littleton, Hugh

HUDSON, Hattie B.   Feb 6, 1902
  See Decker, Andrew F.

HUDSON, Huse   8 Years Ago   Dec 12, 1901
  September 16, 1893 Huse Hudson and Miss Leona Tuxford, of Big Neck, were
  married.

HUDSON, Lizzie   Apr 24, 1897
  See Haines, James   (For correction see Hynes, Wakeman)

HUDSON, Miss Mollie   Dec 22, 1898
  See Adams, Isaac

HUDSON, Orves   Camp Point   Apr 12, 1900
  Orves Hudson and Violet Stump were married Tuesday of last week, by
  Rev McNabb. Will live on the Stump farm northwest of town.

HUEY, Walter   Augusta   Dec 20, 1900
  Walter Huey and Miss Abbey Young were married at the residence of the bride
  parents last Wednesday evening by Elder A.L. Ferguson. Only the immediate
  relatives of the parties were present. They left at 8 o'clock for Ex-
  celsior Springs, Missouri, where they visited over Sunday. The bride is
  the daughter of H.W. Young and wife and is one of Augusta's best young
  ladies. She had charge of room 3 in our public school for seven continuous
  years, and is prominent in church work, being the leading soprano in the
  Christian church choir. The groom is an excellent young business man,
  and one of the proprietors of the Cannon and Huey meat market. He is a
  thorough gentleman. They will reside in Augusta.

HUFF, George   Long Courtship   Feb 28, 1901
  After a courtship over a period of 35 years, George Huff age 58 years,
  a well to do farmer living 8 miles east of Plymouth was Thursday married
  to Miss Callie Wilburn, age 54 of this neighborhood. Huff began keeping
  company with Miss Wilburn when she was 19 years old. "Quincy Whig"

HUFF, Mrs Laura E.   Cards are out   Dec 22, 1898
  Cards have been issued from this office for the marriage of Mrs Laura E.
  Huff and Rev James M. Duff. Wedding will be at brides home Wednesday eve
  December 28th. Rev Duff is pastor of the ME Church at Literberry, Illinois

HUFF, Mrs Laura E.   Dec 22, 1898
  See Duff, Rev James M.

HUGHES, Miss Alma B.   Nov 14, 1901
  See Laughlin, George A.

HUGHES, Horace Eben   Local   Aug 7, 1903
  At the ME Parsonage in this village Wednesday eve, Horace Eben Hughes, of
  Augusta and Miss Letha Viola Balfour of Pine Grove were married by Rev
  Fuller.

HUGHES, John   Local   Jul 10, 1897
  John Hughes, a former LaPrairie boy, but who now resides in Quincy, was
  married at Olanthe, Kansas last week to Miss Bertha Lemmon. Will live
  Quincy.

HUGHES, Mary B.   March 18, 1893   Apr 18, 1901
  See Hackney, Wm D.

HUGHES, Miss Myrtie   Local   Jun 24, 1904
   Miss Myrtie Hughes, of Bowen, left Tuesday for St Paul and on her arrival
   was married to George W. Rhea, who is a son of Lon Rhea, formerly lived
   here. Mr Rhea has for some time held a position as telegraph operator at
   Bemidji, Minnesota and with his bride will live there. Bride is daughter
   of Mr and Mrs W.F. Hughes who at one time live here, but now reside near
   Bowen.
HUGHES, Miss Viola   Dec 19, 1902
   See Wolff, Anton Conrad
HUGHLETT, Miss Nancy   Nov 4, 1904
   See Stump, Roy
HUISMAN, Klaus and Mary   Local   Jul 4, 1896
   Evidence was taken Wednesday in circuit court in the divorce case of
   Klaus Huisman vs Mary Huisman and the defendents request for provisional
   alimony was granted.
HUISMAN, Klaus   Dec 19, 1896
   See Jurgens, Miss Maggie
HUISMAN, Mrs Ricka   May 17, 1900
   See Friedricks, Christian
HULL, Miss Bertha   Sep 25, 1902
   See McHatton, Win
HULTS, George   Local   Feb 13, 1897
   George Hults and Miss Emma Poppie were married at Carthage, Tuesday.
HUNSAKER, Orval   May 30, 1901
   See Garrett, Miss Grace and Jennie
HYDE, Charles E.   Oct 16, 1897
   See Rose, Miss Nellie
IHMEN, John J.   January 1893   Jan 24, 1901
   January 28 Marriage license issued to John J. Ihmen and Miss Hienke Post
   of Clayton.
IHRIG, John H.   Locals   Mar 24, 1905
   John H. Ihrig and Miss Mildred Blanche Callahan of Camp Point, were mar-
   ried at the Callahan home in Camp Point at noon Wednesday. John is son of
   Mr and Mrs Geo. Ihrig, of near Golden. Will live on the Ihrig farm.
INCE, Jim   Camp Point   Mar 20, 1902
   Jim Ince and Miss Addie McCaffery were married at the brides home on Sun-
   day eve last.
IRVIN, Sarah C.   Jan 23, 1903
   See Craig, George
IRVIN, Wm   York Neck   May 12, 1905
   That long looked for wedding came off last week, the contracting parties
   were Wm Irvin and Miss Ida Mix. Will live on old Irvin homestead.
IRWIN, Miss Ora   Jan 24, 1898
   See Griggs, Geo.
IRWIN, Miss Ora M.   Married   Jun 24, 1898
   Wednesday eve June 15th occured the marriage of Miss Ora M. Irwin and
   George Griggs, of Bowen. Both, especially the birde is well known in
   Golden. Mr Griggs is in business at Adrian where they will live.
ISENSE, Oscar   Local   Oct 13, 1898
   Rev Chas. Wehrman, left on Monday for Edwardsville, where he was called to
   solomnize the marriage of Oscar Isense of Chicago and Miss Minnie Vollroth
   of Edwardsville.
JACKSON, May   Feb 7, 1901
   See Carper, Melvin

JACOBS, Miss Ada   Sep 14, 1899
  See Willard, Hurley F.
JACOBS, Miss Alta   5 Years Ago   Aug 7, 1897
  Miss Alta Jacobs was married to Arthur Ferman, at the ME Church in this cit
JACOBS, Cora May   Mar 16, 1898
  See Keeney, John B.
JACOBS, Miss Nettie   5 Years Ago   Feb 20, 1897
  See Detmers, George
JACOBS, Samuel and Martha   Local   Oct 17, 1896
  Samuel Jacobs, of Columbus, does not care for further association with his
  wife, Martha. They were married away back in 1867, but love has grown cold
  They seperated December 20, 1895. She now lives at West Point, Illinois
  Hancock County the husbands bill for divorce was filed by attorneys
  Vandeventer and Montgomery Thursday. Extreme and repeated cruelty are the
  grounds for action.
JAMES, Miss Margaret   June 16, 1894   Jul 24, 1902
  See Hedrick, Dr E.G.
JAMISON, Thomas   Pea Ridge   Apr 5, 1896
  Married at the court house in Mt Sterling, Thomas Jamison and Miss Emma
  Mixsell Wednesday eve of last week. They will live in Clayton.
JANSEN, Miss Flora E.   Mar 4, 1904
  See Miller, John H.
JANSEN, Miss Tena   Mar 5, 1904
  See Miller, John
JANSSEN, Albertus   To Be Married   Mar 1, 1900
  Tonight at 8 PM in the West Side Lutheran Church will occur the marriage of
  Albertus Janssen to Miss Emma H. Eigenberg by Rev Alpers. Groom will be
  attended by William Janssen and John H. Utesch while Maggie and Alvina
  Eigenberg, sisters of the bride will be bridesmaids. Supper will be
  served at home of brides parents afterwards. Both are members of the
  West Side Lutheran Church. Bride is daughter of John Eigenberg and wife.
  Groom is son of Heinrich Janssen and is a book-keeper at Peoples Exchange
  Bank, a graduate of Gem City Business College.
JANSSEN, Etha C.   Mar 7, 1901
  See Reuschal, Henry F.
JANSSEN, Miss Etha C.   Mar 14, 1901
  See Reuschel, Henry F.
JANSSEN, George   Married   Apr 5, 1900
  Tonight at the West Side Lutheran Church will occur the marriage of George
  Janssen and Miss Margaret Buss at 7:30, two of Goldens young people. Miss
  Margaret Emminga will act as bridesmaid and Miss Margaret Tansman, of
  Quincy will be maid of honor. John Buss will be best man and William
  Janssen as groomsman, while H. Osterman and A. Harberts will be ushers.
  Bride will be given away by her father, W.J. Buss. Reception will be at
  brides parents after ceremony. Both are members of the West Side Church.
  Will live in west part of town.
JANSSEN, George   Married   Apr 12, 1900
  Married, George Janssen and Miss Margaret Buss last Thursday eve in the
  West Side Lutheran Church at 8 PM. John Buss escorted the groom to the
  alter. Bride was given away by her father, supper was served at the home
  of brides parents.
JANSSEN, Miss Mary   Oct 16, 1903
  See Goosman, John R.
JENKENS, Miss Mattie   Feb 13, 1897
  See Orr, Layfayette

JENKINS, Lizzie   Texas   Aug 26, 1904
  Lizzie Jenkins and George Nutt, of Loraine were married Thursday.
JEWELL, Miss Gertie   Local   Apr 24, 1897
  Miss Gertie Jewell and Lon Boger were married at Camp Point Wednesday.
JEWELL, Miss Gertrude   May 1, 1897
  See Boger, Lawrence
JEWETT, Miss Nettie   Dec 5, 1902
  See Hoke, John H.
JOHNSON, Miss Carrie   Jun 3, 1904
  See Bower, George H.
JOHNSON, Miss Emily M,   Jul 8, 1898
  See Cockern, John S.
JOHNSON, Mrs Flora   May 10, 1900
  See Miller, John
JOHNSON, Fred   Jun 14, 1900
  See Fink, Miss Gussie
JOHNSON, Mr Geo.   Feb 24, 1905
  See Gronewold, Miss Anna
JOHNSON, Geo.   Local   Mar 3, 1905
  Mr Geo. Johnson, of Peoris, and Miss Anna Gronewold were married at Trinity
  Lutheran Church Sunday at 6:30 PM. Dinner served at Gronewold home to
  invited guests.
JOHNSON, H.C.   May 31, 1900
  See Hawley, Miss Nettie
JOHNSON, Miss Laura E.   Dec 26, 1901
  See Heinecke, Charles
JOHNSON, Pink   Pea Ridge   Aug 31, 1899
  Pink Johnson, our jolly good neighbor, hied himself away to Lewiston last
  week where he married Miss Pearl Crawford, daughter of our former pastor,
  Elder Crawford. Marriage took place Sunday at the family home in Lewiston.
JONES, Guy   Local   Jun 26, 1903
  Guy Jones, of Seattle, Washington, and Miss Allie McNeil, of Versailles,
  were married in Seattle June 2nd. Bride was reared in Versailles and
  groom grew to manhood in this place.
JONES, J.C.   Married   Aug 5, 1904
  At the dawn of early morning Sunday our friend, J.C. Jones, who so recently
  came among us packed his grip and stole away to call on his folks at
  St Louis. The St Louis Republic of August 2 announces: Marriage of Mr
  Jones to Miss Edna D. Sams of Brighton, Illinois, Mr Jones native town, at
  the Planters Hotel in St Louis, on the AM of August 1st. Mr and Mrs Jones
  arrived Tuesday eve to make their home among us. Will live in residence
  of W.J. Buss.
JONES, John W.   May 19, 1905
  See Davis, Miss Laura Bell
JONES, Laura   Augusta   Nov 3, 1898
  Laura Jones of this place and Samuel Lewis of Plymouth were married at the
  depot on last Thursday eve at 9. Will live Plymouth.
JONES, Miss Pearl   Oct 21, 1904
  See Carter, David W. and William T.   (double wedding)
JOPMANN, Mr and Mrs John   Local   Dec 5, 1902
  Henry H. Flesner and Anna meints, also John Buss of Chatton, started Tues-
  day night for Gage County Nebraska where they will attend the golden wed-
  ding of Mr and Mrs Jopmann.
JOSEPH, Miss   Camp Point   Dec 1, 1898
  Mr and Mrs Arthur Vandoren came up from Quincy to attend the wedding of her
  sister, Miss Joseph.

JOSEPH, Miss Fannie   Jun 5, 1897
    See Piper, Clay
JOSEPH, Miss Florence   Dec 1, 1898
    See Dehaven, Will
JOSLIN, Bertrice E.   Married at Galesburg   Dec 20, 1902
    On Thursday of last week at Galesburg,Bertrice E. Joslin, of Farmington,
    Illinois and Miss Urith Selby, of this village, were married by a Meth-
    odist minister at his home in that city. Mrs Robert McCray and Miss Edith
    Selby, accompanied the bride to Galesburg and were present at the wedding.
    Mr and Mrs Nevins, of Burlington, Iowa and Mrs Clara Rhea, of Galesburg
    were also present. After ceremony the young couple left for Farmington,
    Illinois where Mr Joslin is employed as a telegraph operator and where
    they will make their home. Both were reared in Golden. Groom being for
    a time employed at the New Era.office. Later he studied telegraphy and
    now has a good position.
JOSLIN, Mrs Mary E.   Married   Dec 28, 1895
    Thursday, December 26th Mrs Mary E. Joslin of this place was married to
    J.C. Nevius of Burlington, Iowa at the Vermont St. ME Church at Quincy
    at 11:30 by pastor Rev G.A. Scott. Bride was born and reared in this
    vicinity. Groom is traveling salesman for a Burlington house. Will
    live Burlington.
JUILFS, Dick   5 Years Ago   Nov 13, 1897
    Dick Juilfs and Miss Kate Buhr were married at the home of Cobus Buhr.
JUNK, Edwin   Married   Nov 13, 1897
    Married last Wednesday eve at 5 at the home of the brides parents, south
    of town, Mr Edwin Junk and Miss Sarah Gooding by Rev A.B. Peck of the
    ME Church. Wedding supper served by sisters of the bride. Will live
    with their parents the coming winter. "Bowen Chronicle"
JURGENS,   Feb 27, 1897
    See Bachman,
JURGENS, Miss Annie   Local   Feb 27, 1897
    Married at West Side German Church Wednesday eve, Miss Annie Jurgens to
    J.F. Harbor, of Augusta by Rev Alpers. Bride is daughter of townsman
    J.J. Jurgens and is the second of his daughters to be married this week.
JURGENS, Christian   Feb 2, 1899
    See Miller, Miss Rena Elisabeth
JURGENS, John Jr.   Married   May 3, 1900
    Married, one of Golden's young men, John Jurgens Jr and Miss Mattie Eckhof
    of Damon at the German Lutheran Church at Damon on April 8th by Rev Jerken
    Bride is daughter of Hye Eckhoff. Couple moved to Golden about ten days
    ago and located in the south part of town.
JURGENS, Miss Lizzie   Married   Feb 27, 1897
    Married Tuesday at 3 PM, Miss Lizzie Jurgens of Golden to Mr Wm Bachman,
    of Elvaston at the German Lutheran Church, in Hamilton by Rev Rusze.
    Wedding feast afterwards at grooms parents near Elvaston. Bride is dau-
    ghter of J.J. Jurgens who lives south part of town. Will live Elvaston.
JURGENS, Miss Maggie   Married   Dec 19, 1898
    Married, at the home of Rev Best, First and Goodwin Sts. Peoria, Illinois
    Thursday eve December 11th Klaus Huisman and Miss Maggie Jurgens. Mr
    Huisman is one of our popular german friends and is traveling for an
    Indianapolis Hardware firm. Bride is daughter of J.J. Jurgens, of this
    place, Will live in this city.
JURGENS, Miss Marie   Aug 9, 1900
    See Marsh, Henry

JURGENS, Miss Mary   Feb 6, 1902
    See Thompson, George
KEENEY, John B.   Local   Mar 16, 1898
    John B. Keeney of Nelleton, Missouri and Cora May Jacobs were married at the
    home of Mrs Emily Jacobs, about six miles northwest of Golden, on last
    Wednesday at high noon by Rev Wehrman. Will live at Nelleton, Missouri.
KELLER, Miss Rosa   Jun 1, 1904
    See McHatton, Ambrose
KELLEY, Alfonzo   Jun 10, 1898
    See Duis, Miss Lena
KELLEY, Alva   May 27, 1898
    See Duis, Miss Lena
KELLEY, Mrs Annie F.   Apr 14, 1905
    See Gay, Charles V.
KERN, Miss Anna   Jan 15, 1904
    See Beringer, Fred
KESSLER, Miss Stella   Mar 27, 1902
    See Reynolds, John
KESTING, Miss Darlia   Sep 25, 1903
    See Little, George F.
KETCHUM, Miss Francis L.   Jan 2, 1897
    See Leidy, Rev J.M.
KETCHUM, Miss Neva   Oct 20, 1905
    See Eary, Ray
KETCHUM, Vivian   Augusta   Dec 6, 1900
    Ed McAfee and wife attended wedding of Mrs McAfee's brother, Vivian Ketchum
    to Miss Jessie Thompson, in Galesburg, last Thursday.
KILEY, Mrs Mary   LaPrairie   Dec 12, 1901
    Mrs Mary Kiley, of Quincy, was guest of her sister, Miss Jennie McClain,
    several days last week.
KIMBALL, Miss Pearl   Aug 5, 1904
    See Miller, Carl
KIMBALL, Miss Rosa   March 8, 1894   Mar 30, 1899
    See Ford, Ed
KINCHELOE, C.F.   Easter Wedding   Apr 24, 1897
    Loraine, April 19th, wedding of Hon. C.F. Kincheloe and Miss Flora Michel
    took place in Christian Church yesterday at high noon by Rev J.M. Ruby
    of Quincy.
KINCHLOE, H.E.   York Neck   Sep 4, 1903
    Married at Springfield, August 23, 1903, H.E. Kinchloe, of Loraine, to
    Miss Bertha E. Beer of York Neck. Mr Kinchloe is principal of the
    Fowler school.
KINDHART, Miss Dora   Nov 10, 1905
    See Clark, Charles
KINDHART, Miss Hannah   Elm Grove   Aug 28, 1902
    Miss Hannah Kindhart who has been making her home with Ira Reynold's family
    for about three months, left Monday eve of last week in company with
    William Shepherd and they were married on Tuesday in Mt Sterling.
KING, Miss Ida   Sep 20, 1900
    See Maddox, Dr.
KING, Miss Jomattie   Apr 18, 1898
    See Hecox, Oscar
KING, Mr Lawrence   Jul 17, 1902
    See Willard, Miss Ella
KING, Miss Lydia   Jun 16, 1905
    See Wallace, Richard A.

KIRBY, Albert   Augusta   Jul 5, 1900
Relatives here have received invitations to the marriage of Albert Kirby
which takes place Thursday in Ohio. He visited here last April and May
at the home of Elder Ferguson.

KIRKLAND, Frank   Augusta   Jan 18, 1900
Married yesterday, Frank Kirkland of Rome, New York and Miss Helen Newcomb
daughter of P.P. Newcomb and wife of this place at the family home by
Dr. Sanderson. Will live New York, groom vistied here frequently during
the lifetime of his former wife, Abbie Newcomb, sister of Miss Helen.
He is a merchant at Rome. Bride was born and raised here in Augusta.
Was teacher in our public school several years ago.

KLEM, Will   Camp Point   Feb 22, 1900
Last Thursday at 9:30 PM Will Klem and Miss Lula Harris were married by
Elder Dilley at his place of business. Will live on a farm 4½ miles
northeast of town.

KLEPPER, Clyde E.   Local   Dec 4, 1897
Marriage license issued for marriage of Clyde E. Klepper, of Augusta and
Miss Jessie Ganz of LaPrairie.

KLOSS, George   Camp Point   May 31, 1900
On Thursday of this week George Kloss will be married to a young lady in
Kansas. We have not learned her name.

KNIGHT, Miss Anna   Mar 6, 1902
See Lubben, Jurgen H.

KNIGHT, Charley   Sulphur Springs   Jan 23, 1902
Charley Knight and Miss Katie Toach were married Wednesday eve of last
week at the home of Wm Lambert.

KNIGHT, Dent   May 1, 1897
See McClain, Alfred

KOETZLE, Miss May   Dec 4, 1903
See Thompson, William

KOHLMAN, Barney   Local   Oct 9, 1897
Barney Kohlman, of Glenville, Nebraska and Miss Ida Miller, of this place,
were married at the home of the bride, Thursday afternoon by Rev Dorrow.
Bride is daughter of Chris Miller. Barney is son of Herman Kohlman and for
many years a resident of this place. Will live Glenville.

KOONTZ, Charles   La Prairie   Dec 16, 1904
John Koontz, of Quincy, came home Thursday to attend wedding of his brother
Charles.

KOONTZ, Charles   LaPrairie   Dec 23, 1904
Thursday, December 8th, at the home of brides parents occurred the marriage of Charles Koontz and Miss Effie Calkins. Last Friday a reception
was given at the future home of the couple by Miss Della, sister of the
groom who assisted her brother in furnishing and preparing the cozy little
home for the immediate reception of the bride.

KOONTZ, Miss Della   LaPrairie   Nov 10, 1905
Cards are out announcing the wedding of Miss Della Koontz, of LaPrairie,
to Charles P. Miller, of Big Neck, Wednesday eve November 8th.

KOONTZ, Miss Della   Married   Nov 10, 1905
Married at the home of Mrs M. Koontz, 1½ miles northeast of LaPrairie
Wednesday eve November 8, 1905, Miss Della Koontz, of LaPrairie and Mr
Charles Miller, of Big Neck at 6 PM by Rev Ross of LaPrairie. Otho Arnold
of Quincy sang "O Promise Me" and wedding march was played by Mrs Otho
Arnold. Bride and groom attended by Miss Maud Gibbs, of Mendon and John
Koontz, brother of the bride. Newly wedded couple left on Eli for Pennsyl-
vania to visit groom's mother and other relatives for several weeks. will
live after Jan. 1st, 1906, 1½ miles east of Big Neck.

KOONTZ, Ray L.   Local   Dec 25, 1903
    A marriage license issued on Wednesday to Ray L. Koontz and Miss Ethel A.
    Brown of Camden.
KRIEBLE, Ella   Jul 11, 1896
    See Phillips, Luke
LAIRD, Miss Matilda   Oct 16, 1897
    See Gibson, Joseph H.
LAMBERT, Mr   Marcelline   Oct 10, 1896
    A wedding at Marcelline last Sunday night, a Mr Lambert, of Quincy and
    Miss Vina Shepherd, of this place.
LAMBERT, Dr   From old New Era's   Jul 24, 1902
    June 23, 1894 Dr Lambert, of Coatsburg, and Miss Nellie Carlin, of Bowen,
    were married.
LAMMA, Sherman   Hebron   Sep 29, 1905
    This vicinity was surprised by hearing of the marriage of Sherman Lamma and
    Miss Lottie McClintock which occurred at Quincy Saturday afternoon.
LANCE, Joe   Clayton   Aug 22, 1896
    A quiet wedding took place here Thursday eve, Joe Lance and Miss Hattie
    Downing. Will live Chicago.
LANERTS, Klaus   Married   Jan 30, 1897
    Sunday January 24th occurred the marriage of Klaus Lanerts and Miss Martha
    Buss at the East Side German Church by Rev Dorrow.
LANERTS, Klaas O.   Local   Jan 16, 1897
    Marriage license has been issued to Klaas O. Lanerts and Miss Martha G.
    Buss, both of Golden.
LANERTS, Rank O.   Jan 8, 1898
    See Detmers, Miss Tena
LANNING, Miss Hattie   Local   Aug 14, 1897
    Miss Hattie Lanning and James Caffery, of York Neck, were married.
LANDSTROME, Mabel   Fairview   Jul 4, 1901
    Married at the home of brides parents at high noon Wednesday, Mabel
    Landstrome to O.L. McCann of Helena, Montana by Rev M.S. McCoy. Guests
    were present from Monroe City, Missouri, Galesburg, Illinois, Carthage,
    Illinois and St Louis, Missouri.
LANTICE, William   Camp Point   Feb 9, 1899
    William Lantice and Mrs Matilda Courtney were quietly married Wednesday at
    6 PM by Elder Dilley.
LARONT, Annie   Jun 15, 1899
    See Pearce, Lyman
LARONT, Miss Annie   Jun 22, 1899
    See Pearce, Lyman
LARONTE, Miss Clara   Oct 17, 1901
    See Sweikert, Wm
LARONTE, Miss M. Lena   Wedding   Apr 22, 1904
    On Thursday eve, April 14th at 8 PM at the home of Mr and Mrs J.S. LaRonte,
    in York Neck, occurred the marriage of their daughter, Miss M. Lena to
    Lawrence E. Turner of Loraine by Rev C.S. Baughman. Will live Cedar
    Rapids, Iowa.
LAUGHLIN, Arthur   Camp Point   Dec 22, 1898
    Rev T.M. Dillen will go to Augusta December 27th to perform ceremony that
    will make Arthur Laughlin and Maude DeGroot man and wife, they will be
    married in the ME Church at 6 PM.

LAUGHLIN, George A.   Married   Nov 14, 1901
   George A. Laughlin and Miss Alma B. Hughes, of this village, were married
   on Wednesday of last week at Hotel Dudley, Palmyra, Missouri. Both have
   lived Golden for a number of years. Will be at home to friends after
   December 1st in the house recently left vacant by Irwin Beckett.

LAWLESS, Mr   Jan 8, 1898
   See Aaron, Miss Edna

LAWLESS, Anna   Dec 22, 1898
   See Thansmidt, Fred

LAWLESS, Wm B.   Local   Jan 1, 1898
   This office last week printed wedding invitations for marriage of Wm B.
   Lawless and Miss Edna V. Aaron, of near Big Neck which occured on the
   29th inst.

LEACH, Miss Daisy   Oct 24, 1896
   See Emery, Olin

LEACH, Francis L.   Local   Feb 12, 1904
   Francis L. Leach and Miss Louisa M. Gilbert of Coatsburg were married
   this week.

LEAR, Mrs Anna   Jul 1, 1904
   See Callahan, Matthew Wesley

LEE, Miss Alice   Nov 8, 1900
   See Akers, Mr Ira

LEENERTS, Miss Helkea   Mar 11, 1904
   See Gronewold, William

LEENERTS, Leenert   Locals   Feb 24, 1905
   Our old friend Leenert Leenerts has taken himself a wife in the person of
   Mrs Engelina Franken of this place. Marriage took place at Trinity Church
   at 10 AM Thursday by Rev Hugo Dorrow.

LEENERTS, Lena   Feb 6, 1903
   See Goudshall, Gottlieb

LEENERTS, Miss Lena   Feb 13, 1903
   See Goudschal, Gottlieb

LEENERTS, Rank   Feb 15, 1900
   See Schone, Miss Lena

LEES, Sallie and Thomas   Local   Dec 14, 1899
   Sallie Lees was granted a divorce from Thomas Lees last week. The couple
   formerly resided in Big Neck.

LEHROFF, Hye   Local   Sep 9, 1904
   On last Sunday AM at 9:30 at the East Side German Lutheran Church, occurred
   the marriage of Hye Lehroff, of Golden, and Anna Fruken, daughter of Dick
   Fruken of this place by Rev Darow. John Gerdes was best man and Mary
   Lehroff, sister of groom was bridesmaid. Will live on a farm northwest
   of Golden.

LEHROFF, Miss Lizzie   Oct 27, 1905
   See Paben, John E.

LEIDY, Rev J.M.   5 Years Ago   Jan 2, 1897
   Rev J.M. Leidy and Miss Francis L. Ketchum were married at LaPrairie.

LEIFINGHOUSE, Louis   Local   Aug 25, 1898
   Wednesday eve at 6, Louis Leifinghouse and Miss Laura McClintock were
   married at the home of Mrs E.A. McClintock. Bride was born and raised
   near Golden.

LEMMON, Asabel   Local   Jun 14, 1900
   Marriage license was issued Monday to Asabel Lemmon, of Quincy, and Miss
   Annie Crabbie, of Loraine.

LEMMON, Miss Bertha   Jul 10, 1897
   See Hughes, John
LEMMON, Mr and Mrs R.   Loraine   Jan 15, 1898
   Mr and Mrs R. Lemmon celebrated their 25th wedding anniversary about
   December 15th.
LEMMONS, R.W. (Whit)   Ursa   Dec 11, 1897
   R.W. Lemmons, a former Ursa boy has returned here, and will open a barber
   shop in Dr Worley's office building. Whit was just married Thanksgiving
   day. His wife and mother in law are now in the east visiting. After
   terminating their visit his wife will come here, where they will live
   till next spring.
LENERT, Klaas   Elm Grove   Jan 30, 1897
   Klaas Lenert was reported to have been married Sunday at the German Church
   in Golden.
LENERTS, Renke B.   Feb 8, 1900
   See Schone, Lina
LEOFFEL, John   Dec 24, 1896
   See Forest, Miss Maggie
LEVY, Joseph   Round about us   Jun 20, 1896
   Monday two strangers came to Warsaw, giving their names as Joseph Levy of
   Quincy and Helen A. Elliot. They wanted to get married and one Tuesday
   eve were married by Squire D.H. Cox, at the city hall. It so happened
   that several persons recognized the groom as Louis Lyons, of Keokuk and
   are wondering why the assumed name. Warsaw Bulletin
LEWIS, Miss   Nov 9, 1895
   See McDowell, Moses
LIERLE, Miss Bessie   Clayton   Jan 29, 1898
   Rev E.R. Lierle has gone to Norwalk, Iowa to visit relatives where he will
   perform the ceremony uniting his granddaughter, Miss Bessie Lierle, daughter
   of I.A. Lierle, to Mr Willett.
LIGHTBODY, Thomas and May   Houston   Sep 19, 1901
   Misses Eliza and Mary Donley and Rosa Wartick returned Saturday from Mis-
   souri where they attended the double wedding of their cousins, Thomas and
   May Lightbody.
LITTLE, George F.   Local   Sep 25, 1903
   George F. Little, of Quincy and Miss Darlia Kesting, of Clayton were mar-
   ried at Clayton Wednesday. Groom is a switchman for the Wabash R.R. and
   formerly lived near Clayton.
LITTLETON, Elnore M.   Local   Nov 27, 1902
   Marriage license was issued Tuesday to Elnore M. Littleton, of Loraine,
   and Ella Miller, of Mendon. Bride was 15 years old.
LITTLETON, Hugh   York Neck   Mar 16, 1899
   Married Wednesday, Hugh Littleton and Annie Hudson, of Big Neck.
LITTLETON, Hugh   Loraine   Mar 16, 1899
   Marriage of Mr Hugh Littleton and Miss Hudson during the past few days.
LITTLETON, Hugh   Big Neck   Mar 16, 1899
   Hugh Littleton, of Loraine and Miss Anna Hudson, of Big Neck were married
   at Esq. Reece's Wednesday the 8th.
LOGSDEN, Lillie   Neighborhood   Jun 12, 1897
   Married at Mt Sterling last week, pretty little Lillie Logsden, age 15
   and Charlie F. Friday age 19 by Parson Madden Wednesday evening with both
   mama's consent.

LOOMILLER, John C.   Married   Dec 25, 1897
  A dispatch from Princeton, Indiana says John C. Loomiller and Mrs Martha
  Cosby of Hazelton, Indiana were married Thursday. Loomiller is the blind
  man whose wife and niece were murdered in Liberty township some four
  years ago.

LORIMER, Rev M.W.   Local   May 25, 1899
  Rev M.W. Lorimer has received invitation to the marriage of his brother,
  who was here last July and preached at the Presbyterian Church. Wedding
  will be in the North Buffalo Church, Pennsylvania of which Rev Lorimer
  is pastor and of which the lady, Miss Anna Knox, is a member on Tuesday,
  May 30th at 10:30 AM. Bride and groom will tour West and be in Monmouth
  at the home of groom's parents and possibly a few days in Golden. Will
  live parsonage at Buffalo, Pennsylvania after July 11th.

LORIMER, Rev M. Wallace   Wedding   Sep 25, 1897
  Married at noon today at home of Rev and Mrs Andrew Renwick, 508 N. Second
  Street, when their daughter, Miss Maude and Rev M. Wallace Lorimer of
  Golden. They were attended by Rev W.M. Lorimer of Xemia cemetery, the
  grooms brother and Miss Daisy Renwick, the brides sister. Vows spoken
  by Rev A. Renwick, the brides father and Rev S.W. Lorimer, the grooms
  father offered the prayer. Both Rev and Mrs Lorimer received their edu-
  cation in Monmouth College. Will live Golden where groom has just been
  installed pastor of the United Presbyterian Church.
  (Monmouth Daily Review   September 15th.)

LORIMER, Rev M. Wallace   To Be Married   Sep 11, 1897
  New Era received invitation to marriage of Miss Maude Renwick, of Monmouth
  to Rev M. Wallace Lorimer, pastor of the United Presbyterian Church of thi
  place to be at the home of the brides parents September 15th. Rev Lorimer
  left for Monmouth Thursday PM and after wedding will go to the Moody
  Bible Institute at Chicago a few weeks. Will be at home after October 5th

LORIMER, Rev W.M.   Local   Jun 8, 1899
  Rev W.M. Lorimer and his bride, of Buffalo, Pennsylvania, will arrive at
  the home of Rev M.W. Lorimer next Saturday eve and will spend several days
  with the pastor of our Presbyterian Church.

LOUDERBACK, Iva   Dec 26, 1901
  See Hester, Wm

LUBBEN, Anna   Apr 10, 1897
  See Behrens, Ulfert

LUBBEN, John   Sulphur Springs   Nov 9, 1899
  We understand that John Lubben had quite a wedding at his place last Thurs

LUBBEN, John H.   Local   Nov 2, 1899
  John H. Lubben and Tina Gerjets both of Golden, were licensed to wed Thurs
  day of last week.

LUBBEN, Jurgen H.   Local   Mar 6, 1902
  Squire McCabe yesterday at the office of Alex Hedrick performed the mar-
  riage of Jurgen H. Lubben, of Pea Ridge, and Miss Anna Knight, of Golden.
  "Brown County Republican"

LUCKEL, Albert C.   Apr 21, 1905
  See Funk, Florence Pearl

LUCUS, Charles   Jun 13, 1896
  See Amrine, Bertha

LYDICK, Anna   Nov 27, 1902
  See Woodworth, Stephen

LYONS, Louis   Jun 20, 1896
  See Levy, Joseph

LYONS, Mr and Mrs Louis   Round about us   Jul 18, 1896
    Mr and Mrs Louis Lyons, of Keokuk were in town last week trying to straighten
    out the kinks in the knot the united them under fictitious names. They
    wanted Squire Cox to change the names on the marriage certificate and
    when he wouldn't they went to city clerk Crawford who to please them
    drew up an affidavit on the back of the certificate that they (Louis Lyons
    and Helen Wheeler) were the identical persons to whom the license
    was issued under other names and who were married set forth in the certi-
    ficate and they attached their signatures. "Warsaw Bulletin"
MADDOX, Dr   Augusta   Sep 20, 1900
    Dr Maddox and Miss Ida King, of Augusta were married last week. Dr has
    been a resident of Augusta some six or seven years. Bride has visited here
    during the life time of her sister, the former Mrs Maddox.
MANLOVE, Roy   Local   Oct 30, 1903
    Roy Manlove and Miss Alice Hedrick, of Golden, were married by Rev Parker
    Shields Tuesday afternoon in the parlor of the Tremont Hotel in Quincy.
MARSH, Charles   Jan 8, 1898
    See Heubner, Miss Lena
MARSH, Harry B.   Augusta   Jan 24, 1901
    Harry B. Marsh, of Bowen and Miss Nellie C. Mead were married at the home
    of brides parents, W.H. Mead and wife, last Wednesday at noon by Rev Taylor.
    Left for short visit with Chicago friends. Bride was born and raised in
    Augusta and several years has taught the 3rd grade in our public school,
    resigning the 1st of the year.
MARSH, Henry   Chicago Wedding   Aug 9, 1900
    Chicago, Illinois, August 2   Married at the home of Henry Rath Tuesday
    eve at 8, Henry Marsh and Miss Marie Jurgens, daughter of J.J. Jurgens,
    deceased, of Golden, Illinois by Rev Bolt of the St Jacob Lutheran Church.
MARSHALL, Charles H.   Married   Feb 26, 1904
    Wednesday at 5:30 PM, Charles H. Marshall and Miss Laura E. Beckett were
    married at the ME parsonage in Golden. After ceremony they repaired to
    the home of brides parents for reception. Will live on a farm in York Neck.
MARSHALL, Miss Cora   Nov 23, 1899
    See McClintock, Dave
MARSHALL, Lang   York Neck   Jan 1, 1898
    Married, Wednesday by Rev Collens of Loraine, Mr Lang Marshall and Miss
    Ada McGinely, both of York Neck.
MARSHALL, Leileber   York Neck   Oct 9, 1897
    The long looked for wedding came off Thursday of last week contracting
    parties were Leileber Marshall and Miss Mary Wartick, both of York Neck.
MARSHALL, Lorin   Local   May 6, 1904
    Marriage license issued Monday to Lorin Marshall of Columbus and Miss
    Elfa Boling, of Clayton.
MARTIN, Miss Bessie   Feb 19, 1898
    See Selby, Ralph E.
MARTIN, Mr Charles   Wedding   Mar 31, 1905
    On Tuesday eve of this week at 6 PM at the ME parsonage occurred the wed-
    ding of Mr Charles Martin, of Coatsburg, to Miss Annie Lake Dougherty,
    of Rocky Run, Hancock County. They returned to Coatsburg where Mr Martin
    has been a farmer most of his life, he is 47 years old. Bride is 42 years
    old. They will live near Warsaw.
MARTIN, Miss Rose   Feb 5, 1904
    See Henning, George
MATHENY, Miss Ora L.   Oct 21, 1904
    See Carter, David W. and William T. (double wedding)

MATHEWS, Jennie Mar 16, 1899
 See Cosit, Oliver
MATTHEWS, Miss Anna P. Feb 26, 1904
 See Cain, Lewis L.
MAXWELL, Charles W. Jun 24, 1898
 See Bradney, Miss Belle
MAY, Miss Ella May 1, 1897
 See Shelly, Mr
MAYNARD, Nora Mar 16, 1899
 See Donley, Anderson
MAYSON, Andy Camp Point May 2, 1901
 Andy Mayson and Miss Lizzie Smith were married in the country at the home
 of Rev Perrick Sunday last.
MEAD, Miss Nellie C. Jan 24, 1901
 See Marsh, Harry B.
MEATHERINGHAM, Miss Dessie Jan 23, 1897
 See Omer, Dan
MEINTS, Jurgen J. Sep 8, 1905
 See Schone, Miss Barbara
MEINTS, Wuebke, F. Feb 19, 1904
 See Post, Ludwig
MENSEDIKE, Miss Lillie Oct 5, 1899
 See Bates, Will
MENTZ, Miss Grace Oct 2, 1896
 See Behrens, Ulfert Jr.
MEREDITH, Miss Lutie Augusta May 31, 1900
 Miss Lutie Meredith left Saturday for Tennessee and from there she will go
 to Galesburg Wednesday where she will be married to J.C. Raunels, formerly
 of Canton, Illinois, but now of California. Will leave for a visit to
 Denver, Colorado and live somewhere in the West.
MEYER, Edward H. Local Oct 24, 1901
 Cards are out announcing marriage of Edward H. Meyer to Miss Theda Duis
 at 7 PM October 30th at the East Side Church.
MEYER, Edward H. Married Oct 31, 1901
 Edward H. Meyer and Theda Methea Duis were married at East Side Church at
 7 PM last evening by Rev Darrow. Groom is son of Henry Meyer of this vil-
 lage and bride is daughter of W.D. Duis, proprieter of the Hotel Golden.
 Will live Carthage. Groom is employed as a baker in that city.
MEYER, Mr Frank Jun 19, 1897
 See Harberts, Miss Ollie
MEYERS, Henry Camp Point Mar 19, 1898
 Supplement Henry Meyers of Columbus and Miss Nellie Horner of near this
 place were married at her home last Wednesday eve by Mr Dilley.
MEYERS, Miss Mattie Apr 8, 1898
 See Schriver, Frank
MICHEL, Miss Flora Apr 24, 1897
 See Kincheloe, C.F.
MICKLE, James Augusta Jan 3, 1901
 James Mickel, of Palmyra, Illinois and Miss Cora Young of Bethalto were
 married at the latter place Christmas and are visiting the groom's parents
 Sam Mickel and wife of this place. Groom is an old Augusta boy and is
 located at Palmyra, where he owns a drug store and where they will reside.
MICKLE, Miss Sue Augusta Sep 6, 1900
 Miss Sue Mickle left Tuesday for Duluth, Minnesota and Wednesday eve at
 7 PM she will be married to F.R. Morrison, of that place. She is daughter
 of Barbara Mickle.

MIKESEL, Miss Chloe   Oakwood   May 16, 1901
    Miss Chloe Mikesel and Bert Bulwar were married last Wednesday at the home
    of the brides parents.
MILLER, Widow   Texas   Aug 19, 1904
    Widow Miller, of Loraine and Mr Sligard boarded the train for Quincy last
    Wednesday and returned married.
MILLER, Alexander   Local   Dec 5, 1901
    Alexander Miller and Belle Neal were married on last Thursday, the 28th
    by Rev Wehrman.
MILLER, Alexander   Dec 5, 1901
    See Neal, Miss Belle
MILLER, Miss Anna   Mar 6, 1903
    See Bennett, Tommy
MILLER, Carl   Married   Aug 5, 1904
    Carl Miller, one of our village lads, hied himself to a neighboring town
    took with him a lady fair, went to Carthage and was married. The bride
    is Miss Pearl Kimball, from LaPrairie.
MILLER, Charles   Local   Oct 2, 1903
    Charles Miller and Miss Hetty Aaron, of Big Neck, were married at Quincy,
    Wednesday.
MILLER, Charles   Nov 10, 1905
    See Koontz, Miss Della
MILLER, Charles R.   Nov 10, 1905
    See Koontz, Miss Della
MILLER, Claus   From old New Era's   Sep 18, 1902
    September 8, 1894 Claus Miller and Miss Tena Franzen were married.
MILLER, Ella   Nov 27, 1902
    See Littleton, Elnore M.
MILLER, George   Local   Aug 22, 1901
    Marriage license was issued Monday to George Miller, of LaPrairie and Miss
    Anna Frederick of Golden.
MILLER, George   Henry, Nebraska   Feb 6, 1902
    Married recently, George Miller and Miss Lizzie Thompson.
MILLER, Miss Ida   Oct 9, 1897
    See Kohlman, Barney
MILLER, John   Local   Mar 5, 1904
    John Miller and Miss Tena Jansen were married at the home of the brides
    parents west of Golden Sunday by Rev Dorrow. Will live on a farm near Hulls.
MILLER, John   Augusta   May 10, 1900
    John Miller and Mrs Flora Johnson went to Macomb yesterday afternoon and
    were married. They are both well known here.
MILLER, John H.   Local   Mar 4, 1904
    A marriage license was granted last week to John H. Miller, of Kinderhook,
    and Miss Flora E. Jansen, of Golden.
MILLER, Miss Margaret   Augusta   May 3, 1900
    Married, last Tuesday eve at the home of brides father, Miss Margaret
    Miller to Chas. Browning by Dr Sanderson.
MILLER, Oscar   Local   Jul 31, 1902
    Oscar Miller, of Camp Point and Miss Rosa Wartick, of York Neck, were mar=
    ried last week.
MILLER, Ray   Local   Jan 8, 1904
    At the home of brides parents, Mr and Mrs Wm Downing, in Golden, on Thurs-
    day eve December 31st, Ray Miller and Miss Eva Downing were married by
    Rev Hartley. Will live on the Miller farm west of Golden.

MILLER, Miss Rena Elisabeth   Wierts, Nebraska   Feb 2, 1899
    Married on Monday January 25th at 1 at the German Lutheran Church, Mr
    Christian Jurgens and Miss Rena Elisabeth Miller and returned the home
    to brides parents, Mr and Mrs H.G. Miller. Mrs Henry Hinrichs, sister
    of the bride played the wedding march and then on to their own home the
    next day.
MILLER, Sam   Bethel   Oct 13, 1898
    Sam Miller and Miss Davis, both of Augusta were married at Carthage Septemb
    29th, they made their home with his father and mother.
MILLER, Wm   Review   Jun 12, 1902
    March 3, 1894   Wm Miller, of York Neck, and Sela Garner, of Loraine,
    were married.
MIX, Miss Ida   May 12, 1905
    See Irvin, Wm
MIXSELL, Miss Emma   Apr 5, 1896
    See Jamison, Thomas
MOFFETT, James Renken   Local   Jun 12, 1903
    On Wednesday afternoon Rev McKernon performed the marriage of James Renken
    Moffett, of Clayton and Miss Nellie Bradney, of Paris, Missouri at the home
    of the brides grandparents, Mr and Mrs S.D. Nokes in the vicinity of
    Mounds, Illinois.
MOORE, Miss Anna   Nov 3, 1898
    See Yeldell, Ernest
MOORE, Earnest L.   Apr 24, 1897
    See Selby, Elmer T.   (double wedding)
MOORE, Mrs Mary Jane   Sep 6, 1900
    See Walker, A.J.
MOREY, Miss Stella   Aug 1, 1901
    See Perry, Hon E.A.
MORLEY, Miss Nina   Jun 5, 1902
    See Thomas, Walter
MORRIS, Miss Martha   Mar 7, 1896
    See Woods, George M.
MORRIS, Orvil   Houston   Dec 4, 1897
    Orvil Morris and Miss Lottie Stilwell were married Thursday. We have not
    learned where or the hour.
MORRISON, F.R.   Sep 6, 1900
    See Mickle, Miss Sue
MOTT, Miss Flora   Is Yager a Begimist   Nov 27, 1897
    Silas E. Yager was lodged in our county jail yesterday charged with bigamy.
    He was arrested in Marysville, Missouri and returned. Some weeks ago he
    was united in marriage to Miss Flora Mott of Ferris and is said to have
    previously married one of Marysville's fair daughters.   "Carthage Journal"
MURRAH, Miss Lulu   Mar 11, 1904
    See McCormick, John T.
MURTLE, Miss Electa   Apr 5, 1896
    See Wilkes, Fred
MCADAMS, Arthur F.   Local   Jun 26, 1903
    Arthur F. McAdams and Miss Agnes Pratt, of Loraine, were married this week.
MCANULTY, Mr and Mrs S.R.   Anniversary   Mar 14, 1896
    Saturday March 27th was the 25th wedding anniversary of Mr and Mrs S.R.
    McAnulty.
MCANULTY, S.R.   Local   Mar 21, 1896
    CORRECTION: Last week's article about S.R. McAnulty's wedding anniversary
    a mistake was made in the date of the same which should have been March
    7th also of years married should have been 35.

MCCAFFERY, Miss Addie   Mar 20, 1902
See Ince, Jim
MCCANN, O.L.   Jul 4, 1901
See Landstrome, Mabel
MCCLAIN, Alfred   Pine Grove   May 1, 1897
Alfred McClain and Dent Knight were married Tuesday at the home of brides
sister. They rented a house of Sam Walker and will live there this summer.
MCCLAIN, Miss Jennie   Jan 30, 1903
See Swisher, Bert
MCCLINTOCK, Charles E.   Married   Jun 9, 1905
A home wedding, Thursday, June 1st, Charles E. McClintock and Miss Clara
Floetman at 7:30 PM. Wedding supper followed. Ceremony by Rev W.T.
Reynolds. They will be at home in their newly completed house after
June 10th.
MCCLINTOCK, Dave   Local   Nov 23, 1899
Dave McClintock and Miss Cora Marshall were married at the home of Rev
Wehrman in this village yesterday. Bride is daughter of Thomas Marshall,
of York Neck.
MCCLINTOCK, Miss Effie   Round About Us   Feb 29, 1896
Married Wednesday eve, February 26th at the home of her father, Miss Effie
McClintock to Fred McKinzie of Stillwell, by Rev Charles K. Westfall.
Mr McKinzie will embark in hardware business in Stillwell.
MCCLINTOCK, Miss Jennie   Marriage   Nov 23, 1895
Marriage of Miss Jennie McClintock to Mr Savil H. Eshom occurred at the
home of brides mother, Mrs E.A. McClintock in Houston township, Thursday
eve November 14th by Rev O. Dilley, of Camp Point. Bride was born and
raised in this vicinity.
MCCLINTOCK, Miss Laura   Aug 25, 1898
See Leifinghouse, Louis
MCCLINTOCK, Miss Lottie   Sep 29, 1905
See Lamma, Sherman
MCCLINTOCK, Neva Myrtle   Dec 27, 1900
See Downing, Warren H.
MCCOY, Ralph O.   Local   Apr 1, 1904
Ralph O. McCoy and Miss Tennie Esther Dunant, of Mt Sterling, were married
recently. They located in Mt Sterling where the groom will edit the
Brown County Republican
MCCRAY, Robert J.   5 Years Ago   Dec 26, 1896
Robert J. McCray and Miss Mayme Wallace were married.
MCCUNE, Hughey   Marcelline   Dec 25, 1897
Hughey McCune is now a married man Luenia Adams is the bride.
MCCUNE, John   York Neck   Apr 18, 1901
Wednesday, April 10th occurred the wedding of John McCune, of Loraine to
Miss Anna Aaron, of Big Neck at the home of the bride.
MCDONALD, Mabel   Pine Grove   Nov 14, 1896
Married at the home of Wm McDonald, Wednesday, his daughter, Mabel, to
Wm Eaton, of Huntsville. Mr Eaton is a well to do farmer.
MCDOWELL, Moses   Clayton   Nov 9, 1895
There was a wedding in town Wednesday night Moses McDowell and Miss Lewis.
No cards.
MCFARLAND, Miss Ethel   Jan 9, 1902
See Rutledge, Harley

MCFARLAND, Mr and Mrs John   Anniversary   Dec 1, 1898
    Last Thursday being the 12th anniversary of Mr and Mrs John McFarland's
    marriage, they celebrated in good shape, about 50 people, all the men
    being members of the 100F Lodge at Camp Point of which Mr McFarland is
    a member went out to spend the evening and partake supper. George
    McFarland and sister Miss Sue, furnished the music.
MCFARLAND, Miss Lizzie   Feb 9, 1899
    See Beckett, Clarence E.
MCGARTLAND, Miss Mary   Feb 10, 1905
    See Wheeler, Joel E.
MCGAUGHEY, Charles   Local   Jun 26, 1903
    Charles McGaughey, of Camp Point, and Miss Bertha Omer, of New London,
    Missouri were married this week.
MCGILL, Sydney A.   Local   Sep 27, 1900
    Sydney A. McGill and Eva Pearl Harris were married at the home of the
    brides parents in Houston township Tuesday. Both belong to well to do
    families. After November 1st they will be at home at Bowen, Illinois.
MCGINLEY, Miss Ada   Jan 1, 1898
    See Marshall, Lang
MCGINNIS, Clyde   Augusta   Feb 7, 1901
    Clyde McGinnis and Ina Pearl Beard were married at the home of brides
    parents, T.A. Beard and wife, Wednesday at 6 PM.
MCGINNIS, Harry E.   Exchanges   Dec 2, 1904
    Thursday eve of last week at the home of brides parents occured the mar-
    riage of Harry E. McGinnis and Lizzie M. Neal. Bride is daughter of Mr and
    Mrs James Neal, of Bowen. Groom is son of Mr and Mrs J.L. McGinnis, of
    Big Neck. Will live on farm vacated by Sam Witt.
MCGINNIS, John P.   Feb 1, 1900
    See Robertson, Miss Florence
MCGINNIS, Wm Martin   May 15, 1902
    See Alexander, Fredonia B.
MCHATTON, Ambrose   Local   Jan 1, 1904
    On December 24th at the United Presbyterian parsonage in Golden, Ambrose
    McHatton and Miss Rosa Keller, of this village were married by Rev McKerno
MCHATTON, Miss Irene   Dec 19, 1896
    See Wallace, Chas.
MCHATTON, Win   Local   Sep 25, 1902
    Win McHatton, formerly of Golden, but now of Hulls, and Miss Bertha Hull,
    of that village were married at Barry last Friday. Will live Hulls where
    he is employed as Wabash agent.
MCKINZIE, Fred   Feb 29, 1896
    See McClintock, Miss Effie
MCLEOD, Miss Lizzie   Apr 18, 1901
    See Akers, Mr Posey
MCMULLEN, Miss Ida   Wedding   Jun 10, 1904
    Miss Ida McMullen and Albert Steinert were married at 8 PM Wednesday of
    last week at the home of the brides parents in Keene township by Rev
    W.E. Rose. Only relatives of the young couple were present. Bride is
    daughter of Mr and Mrs A. McMullen of Keene township. Groom is a
    prosperous young farmer of Camp Point. Will got to housekeeping on
    husbands farm.
MCMURRAY, Mrs Mattie   Jun 26, 1902
    See Winston, James M.
MCNEIL, Miss Allie   Jun 26, 1903
    See Jones, Guy

MCWHORTER, Miss May   Nov 21, 1902
    See Aleshire, Wm
NAPIER, Miss Clelia May   May 1, 1903
    See Brink, Oscar Bonney
NASH, Lucian   Apr 1, 1898
    See Norris, Miss Lulu
NATIONS, Dr Guy   Local   Jun 10, 1904
    Dr Guy Nations and Miss Francis Callahan were married.
NEAL, Miss Belle   Big Neck   Dec 5, 1901
    Miss Belle Neal, of Big Neck, and Alexander Miller of Camp Point, were
    married in Camp Point Thursday eve, November 28th.
NEAL, Belle   Dec 5, 1901
    See Miller, Alexander
NEAL, Lizzie M.   Dec 2, 1904
    See McGinnis, Harry E.
NEAL, Mrs Susan   Mar 20, 1897
    See Furgerson, Charles
NEBUR, Miss Kate   Married   May 16, 1896
    Married last Thursday eve at German Lutheran Church on the East Side.
    Miss Kate Nebur and Mr Anton Rosenboom by Rev Darrow. Mr Rosenboom is
    head miller at New Era Mills. Miss Nebur is daughter of the late John Nebur.
NEUMAN, Miss Cora   Mar 13, 1897
    See Burns, Mr
NEVINS, Miss Edith   Aug 31, 1899
    See Omer, Louis
NEVIUS, J.C.   Dec 28, 1895
    See Joslin, Mrs Mary E.
NEWCOMB, Abbie   Jan 18, 1900
    See Kirkland, Frank
NEWCOMB, Miss Helen   Jan 18, 1900
    See Kirkland, Frank
NEWCOMB, Jas. C.   Augusta   Jun 24, 1898
    Married Wednesday eve June 15th Jas. C. Newcomb of this place and Miss
    Florella Whitten of Edgar, Nebraska. Will live Augusta.
NICHOLS, Bert   Local   Feb 26, 1904
    Bert Nichols and Miss Effie Swain, of Loraine, were married last week.
NORRIS, Miss Lulu   Camp Point   Apr 1, 1898
    Miss Maggie Honnold will go to Bowen Wednesday where she will act as
    bridesmaid at the wedding of her cousin, Miss Lulu Norris to Lucian Nash.
NORTH, Miss Lenore   Dec 5, 1902
    See Pratt, Guy
NOYES, Dr F.C.   Round About Us   Jan 11, 1896
    Dr F.C. Noyes of Mt Sterling, and Miss Emma Brierton of Versailles were
    married on Christmas eve.
NUTT, George   Aug 26, 1904
    See Jenkins, Lizzie
O'DELL, Justin   Local   May 15, 1902
    Justin O'Dell, of Bowen, and Miss Nannie Burns, of Peoria County were
    married recently.
ODOR, George   Bowen   Oct 30, 1897
    George Odor and Miss Ida Patchin were married on Wednesday eve. Mr Odor
    lives in Nebraska and Miss Patchin in Bowen.
OETTING, Miss Clara   Dec 20, 1902
    See Eggen, Carl

OGLE, Edward   Oct 23, 1897
    See Bottorff, Mrs Cora
OHNEMUS, Henry   May 9, 1896
    See Cantrell, Miss Laura
OLIVER, Gertrude   Jun 12, 1903
    See Garrett, Peter
OLIVER, Harry   Local   Jun 10, 1904
    Harry Oliver and Miss Edith Robertson were married Wednesday eve at Camp
    Point, on same eve departed for the St Louis exposition.
OMER, Miss Bertha   Jun 26, 1903
    See McGaughey, Charles
OMER, Boom   Camp Point   Sep 21, 1899
    Boom Omer and Miss Maggie De Haven were married by Elder Dilley at his home
    Wednesday eve of last week.
OMER, Miss Cora   5 Years Ago   Jan 22, 1898
    See Bottorff, Anderson
OMER, Miss Cora   January 1893   Jan 3, 1901
    See Bottorff, Anderson
OMER, Cornelius S.   Local   Jan 30, 1903
    On Wednesday eve at 8 at the Methodist Parsonage, Cornelius S. Omer, of
    Camp Point and Miss Jessie Chinn, of Golden, were married by Rev Fuller.
    Groom is a prominent young farmer of his vicinity and bride is daughter
    of Chas. Chinn, our worthy barber. It is understood they will live on
    a farm near Camp Point.
OMER, Dan   Local   Jan 23, 1897
    Dan Omer and Miss Dessie Meatheringham, both of Camp Point were married at
    the parlors of the Tremont House in Quincy, Wednesday.
OMER, Mr and Mrs J. Ed   Local   Mar 21, 1896
    Mr and Mrs J. Ed Omer went to Keokuk Tuesday and were married a second time
    They were married in West Virginia several years ago when Ed was young and
    wild and was sailing under an assumed name. Camp Point Journal
OMER, Louis   Elm Grove   Aug 31, 1899
    Miss Nellie McCord attended the wedding of Louis Omer and Miss Edith Nevins
    at Camp Point last Thursday.
OMER, Miss Myrtle E.   Sep 11, 1903
    See Hostetter, Julian C.
OMER, Pete   Camp Point   Apr 12, 1900
    Pete Omer and Hattie DeHaven were married Wednesday eve of last week.
ORR, Layfayette   Marcelline   Feb 13, 1897
    Layfayette Orr, of Lima and Miss Mattie Jenkens were quietly married last
    week in Quincy.
ORTH, Will   Camp Point   Jan 3, 1901
    Will Orth, of Mendon and Miss Blanche Bradley were married December 25th
    at her home. Only family were present. They left Wednesday for Mendon
    where they will make their home.
ORTON, Daniel   Elm Grove   Apr 5, 1896
    Married, Daniel Orton of Concord township and Miss Conie Robbins in Quincy
    March 18th. Bride is daughter of Jason Robbins.
OSBORN,   Mar 16, 1899
    See Smith, Ruth
OSCHNER, Clarence   Local   May 25, 1899
    Married, Clarence Oschner of La Belle, Missouri and Miss Alta Burke,
    daughter of George W. Burke, of Pine Grove was an event of Bryan day in
    Quincy in the parlors of the St James Hotel. Will live near La Belle, Mo.

OSTERMAN, Anna   Nov 23, 1899
    See Eilers, Nickels
OSTERMAN, Habo   Local   Apr 3, 1903
    Habo Osterman and Miss Tena Weyen were married last Saturday eve by Rev
    Alpers. Will live on the De Groot place, north of town.
OWEN, Miss Effie   Fairview   Oct 10, 1901
    Married at the home of the brides parents, Miss Effie Owen to John W. Young,
    of Bowen, Wednesday at 6 PM by Rev W.A. Taylor. Thursday eve a reception
    was given at the home of grooms parents, Mr and Mrs Young. Will reside on
    Mr Ownes farm near Fairview school house.
OWEN, Miss Ella   Local   Aug 22, 1901
    Whig of yesterday says: Miss Ella Owen of Houston township will be married
    to Darrah Luther Sherrick by Rev A.D. Taylor, of Antioch Church 7 PM this
    evening. Miss Owen is daughter of Chauncey Owen. Mr Sherrick is a young
    farmer of Houston township will live on farm belonging to bride grooms father.
OWEN, Miss Ella   Fairview   Aug 22, 1901
    Cards are out announcing the marriage of Miss Ella Owen to Mr Luther Sherrick
    Wednesday Aug 21, 1901.
OWENS, Edwin   Jun 24, 1904
    See Smith, Leafie'
PABEN, Henry   Local   Oct 21, 1904
    Mr Henry Paben and Miss Kate Herren, both of Golden, were married at Trinity
    Lutheran Church Sunday October 16th. Dinner was served at home of brides
    parents, Mr and Mrs Harm Herren, who live east of Golden. Will live Golden
    in the new home just completed by Mr Paben.
PABEN, John E.   Local   Oct 27, 1905
    John E. Paben and Miss Lizzie Lehroff were married at Trinity Church yest-
    erday at 10 AM. Will live Golden.
PAGE, Paul   Camp Point   May 10, 1902
    Paul Page and Miss Nora Pope were married Thursday eve at brides home.
PARSONS, Miss Ola   May 31, 1900
    See Beckett, Fred
PATCHIN, Miss Ida   Oct 30, 1897
    See Odor, George
PAXTON, Miss Belle   Sep 5, 1901
    See Crook, John
PAXTON, Hayes   Elm Grove   Nov 14, 1896
    Marriage of Mr Hayes Paxton and Miss Elizabeth Steed will be at home of
    brides mother, Mrs Steed Thursday eve by Rev W.H. McDonald, of LaPrairie.
PAXTON, J. Hays   Local   Nov 14, 1896
    License has been issued for marriage of J. Hays Paxton and Miss Elizabeth
    Steed, two of Pine Groves young people. We understand Mr Paxton has rented
    a farm.
PEACOCK, Charles   Jan 1, 1898
    See DeMoss, Miss Bertie
PEARCE, Lyman   Local   Jun 15, 1899
    Marriage license issued Tuesday to Lyman Pearce of Camp Point and Annie
    LaRont, of Golden.
PEARCE, Lyman   York Neck   Jun 22, 1899
    That expected wedding came off Tuesday, Lyman Pearce and Miss Annie Laront
    were the parties, by Esq. Bailey, of Camp Point.
PECK, Royal T.   Married   Jan 20, 1905
    Last Wednesday 6:30 PM, Mr Royal T. Peck and Miss Alma D. Walker were married
    at the brides home. March was played by Sadie Walker. Chas. Walker and
    Jennie Bond were the groomsman and bridesmaid. Rev Adams officiated bride

and groom have known each other from childhood as their families were
neighbors in Illinois. "Local News" Tonkawa, O.T.

PEIL, Henry   Local   May 6, 1898
  Henry Peil and Eva Fowler of Elm Grove were married last week.

PEIL, Miss Martha   Apr 29, 1898
  See Cyzense, Prof. Frank

PEIL, Mrs Tretie   Sep 2, 1904
  See Franzen, Cobus

PERRY, Hon E.A.   Neighborhood News   Aug 1, 1901
  Marriage of Miss Stella Morey, daughter of Mr and Mrs C.H. Morey, of Chicag
  to Hon E.A. Perry of Mt Sterling, at high noon Wednesday, July 24th at the
  home of the brides paretns by Rev J.B. Graver of Jacksonville, a brother
  in law of groom.

PHELPS, Bert   Augusta   Sep 20, 1900
  Last Wednesday at the home of Rev Davidson, Chaplin of the Soldiers Home,
  Bert Phelps and Twila Watts, were married. Bride is daughter of Frank
  Watts and wife of Augusta. Groom is well known here and has always lived
  just east of town in Schuyler County. Will live with grooms parents.

PHILLIPS, Luke   Local   Jul 11, 1896
  About a year ago Luke Phillips of St Marys township, Hancock County was
  married to Ella Krieble, daughter of Geo. Krieble, of this place. Mr
  Phillips rented a farm about three miles west of here of S.L. Fisher.
  This AM Mrs Phillips came home to her father and reported she had left her
  husband, that on yesterday evening he had whipped her with a buggy whip.
  Brooklyn Cor. to Rushville Citizen

PIEL, Fred   Married   Feb 8, 1900
  At the home of the brides parents in Golden last Sunday, Fred Piel and
  Miss Lena Franzen were married at 6 PM by Rev Dorow of the East Side
  German Lutheran Church. Bride is daughter of Harm Franzen.

PIERCE, Mrs Nancy   Apr 27, 1899
  See Fleming, George

PIERCE, Miss Sadie   Feb 15, 1900
  See Cromwell, Thad

PIERCE, Samuel   LaPrairie   Jun 14, 1900
  Married Tuesday eve at the home of brides parents, Samuel Pierce, of Quincy
  to Miss Maud Gans, of this place. Took the train to Quincy where they
  will live.

PILLARS, Riddie   Jan 2, 1897
  See Ferris, John

PIPER, Clay   Camp Point   Jun 5, 1897
  Clay Piper and Miss Fannie Joseph were married at the home of the bride
  Tuesday of last week by Rev A.N. Simmons. Will live in Mt Sterling.

PITTMAN, James J.   Local   May 27, 1904
  James H. Pittman and Miss Olive Garrett, of Camp Point, were married this w

PLATT, Miss Mamie C. Choteau   Jan 28, 1900
  See Stahl, John M.

POLING, Chas.   Married   Apr 10, 1897
  Married at the home of Rev P. Slagle, in this city, Tuesday AM, Chas. Polir
  and Miss Grace E. Stewart, daughter of W.S. Stewart, one of York Neck's
  farmers.

POLING, Eugene P.   Married   Feb 19, 1898
  Mr Eugene P. Poling of Houston township and Miss Harriet E. Downing of Camp
  Point were married at the home of Mr and Mrs Wm Downing last Thursday eve
  at 6 by Rev Wehrman, pastor of the ME Church at Golden. Mr Wm Downing is
  brides father and is one of the oldest settlers in Camp Point township havi
  lived in that township 62 years.

POLING, William B.   Married   May 22, 1903
   At 7 PM Wednesday, William B. Poling and Miss Mary Donley, of this village
   were married by Rev Fuller, Mr Poling holds a good position with the
   Burlington R.R. Will live in north part of town.
PONTIOUS, Mrs Ralph   Exchanges   Feb 6, 1897
   Macombs high tones society is all tore up over divorce suit filed by Mrs
   Ralph Pontious against her husband. They eloped and were married last fall.
POPE, Lenard   Camp Point   May 22, 1897
   Lenard Pope and Emma Snider were married Sunday at 4 PM by Elder Dilly at
   his home.
POPE, Miss Nora   May 10, 1902
   See Page, Paul
POPE, Sam   Camp Point   Jan 12, 1899
   Since our last writing the marriage of Sam Pope and Miss Nell Farlow was
   performed at the home of Squire <u>Baily</u>.
POPPIE, Miss Emma   Feb 13, 1897
   See Hults, George
POST, Albert   Mar 29, 1900
   See Schoene; Miss Mary
POST, Chas. William   Review   Feb 6, 1902
   December 9, 1893   Chas William Post and Miss Catherine Flesner were married
   at Clayton.
POST, Miss Hienke   January 1893   Jan 24, 1901
   See Ihmen, John J.
POST, Miss Lena   Nov 14, 1902
   See Carsteens, Chris
POST, Ludwig   Local   Feb 19, 1904
   A marriage license was issued Tuesday to Ludwig Post and Miss Wuebke F.
   Meints, of Golden.
POST, Miss Mary   Mar 15, 1900
   See Bienhoff, John
POST, Miss Ricke   Feb 26, 1904
   See Flesner, Albert
POST, Miss Rieka   Feb 26, 1904
   See Flesner, Albert
POWELL, Arthur   Married at Bentley   Mar 27, 1902
   The Carthage Gazette of last week says: Marriage of Arthur Powell and Miss
   Grace Burner was Wednesday at 4 PM at the brides home near Bentley. Bride
   is daughter of Geo. Burner and a niece of Mrs A.W. O'Harra of this city.
   Groom is son of F.M. Powell. Reception were held at the home of grooms
   parents yesterday.
POWELL, George W.   Round About Us   Dec 12, 1896
   George W. Powell, of Marcelline, and Miss Essie McMullen, of Mendon came
   to Quincy Monday and were married.   "Quincy Whig"
POWELL, Miss Ida   Jan 23, 1903
   See Sparks, Curtis
PRATT, Miss Agnes   Jun 26, 1903
   See McAdams, Arthur F.
PRATT, Effie   Apr 18, 1901
   See VanHorn, Eugene
PRATT, Guy   Local   Dec 5, 1902
   Guy Pratt, formerly of Loraine, and Miss Lenore North, of Bluffton, Indiana
   were married on Thanksgiving Day.
PRESSLY, Miss Eva   Jun 7, 1900
   See Wysong, Lee

QUEEN, Miss Odessa   Jul 7, 1905
   See Berrier, George
RAHE, Miss Mary   Weyerts, Nebraska   Apr 10, 1897
   First wedding of the season at Mr Rahe's home one mile from Wyerts, where
   Miss Mary Rahe was married to Mr Landgren. Will live Deuel County.
RALEY, Mr Lestie Walter   Sep 9, 1904
   See Akers, Miss Pearl
RALPH, George Jr and Lizzie   Local   Oct 30, 1897
   George Ralph Jr, has sued for divorce from his wife, Lizzie Ralph.
RALPH, Miss Laura   April 15, 1893   Apr 25, 1901
   See Strickler, Jeremiah
RAMSEY, Miss Bertha   Aug 28, 1902
   See Robinson, Arch
RAMSEY, Miss Myrtle   Jun 26, 1903
   See Wartick, John W.
RANDALL, Lewis   Married   Nov 18, 1904
   Correspindence from Lima dated November 14th says, Lewis Randall, of Lorai
   a well known young farmer and Miss Sadie Forsey, of this place left this A
   for Keokuk to be married and expected to return to Loraine this eve in tim
   for supper. Will live near Loraine where Mr Randall farms.
RANDLES, Lawrence A.   Local   Dec 20, 1902
   Lawrence A. Randles, of Mendon and Mary Swain, of Camp Point, were granted
   marriage license this week.
RATHBURN, Miss   Mar 7, 1901
   See Scott, Walter
RAUNELS, J.C.   May 31, 1900
   See Meredith, Miss Lutie
READ, Mary   Mar 7, 1901
   See Coleman, Gabe
REECE, Annie   Mar 19, 1898
   See Runyon, Charles
REED, Henry L.   Jan 5, 1899
   See Gibson, Miss Nellie
REED, Marsh and Bashie   Miserable Married Men   Jul 4, 1896
   One case heard in divorce court was Marsh Reed vs Bashie Reed. Marsh is a
   carpenter and the wife has apparently learned to love others.
REED, Ollie   Nov 27, 1897
   See Hesler, Charles
REEVES, Mrs Malinda   Jan 23, 1902
   See Hoskins, Erastus
REITMAN, Benjamin L.   Jul 11, 1901
   See Schwartz, Miss Mae
RENWICK, Miss Maude   Sep 11, 1897
   See Lorimer, Rev M. Wallace
RESHELL, Polena   Jun 6, 1896
   See Rowe, Henry
REUSCHAL, Henry F.   Local   Mar 7, 1901
   Henry F. Reuschal and Etha C. Janssen, of this place, were licensed to be
   wed yesterday.
REUSCHEL, Henry F.   Local   Mar 14, 1901
   Henry F. Reuschel and Miss Etha C. Janssen, two german people were married
   at the East Side Church last Wednesday eve by Rev Darrow.
REYNOLDS, John   Houston   Mar 27, 1902
   John Reynolds and Miss Stella Kessler of this vicinity were married in
   Quincy on Wednesday of last week by Rev Dana. Groom is son of Geo. Reynol

Sr. and bride is daughter of Chas. Kessler. Will live on the Reynolds
home place.

RHEA, Dick   Dec 1, 1905
See Honnold, Miss Margaret

RHEA. George W.   Jun 24, 1904
See Hughes, Miss Myrtie

RHEA, Miss Grace   Sep 8, 1899
See Blood, Charlie

RHEA, Mrs P.J.   Apr 18, 1896
See Bailey, Thomas

RHEA, Robert C.   Married   Oct 24, 1901
At the home of brides parents in Golden Sunday, at 5 PM Robert C. Rhea and
Clara R. Smith were married by Rev Wehrman. Only near relatives and a few
friends were present. Will live Galesburg where Robert is employed with
the CB & Q Company as a carpenter.

RICE, Miss Connelia   Oct 2, 1903
See Groves, Freeman

RICE, Geo. H.   Married   Feb 1, 1896
6 PM Thursday occurred the marriage of Geo. H. Rice and Miss Myrta Sammends,
daughter of Mr and Mrs J.W. Sammends, of Houston township by Rev O. Dilley
of the Christian Church, Camp Point. Groom is son of John Rice of same
township.

RICE, J.H.   Local   Feb 1, 1900
J.H. Rice and Miss Cora Crum, of Bowen, were married at Quincy Tuesday.

RICHARDSON, Elza   Feb 19, 1904
See Hackney, Miss Nora

RICHARDSON, Elzie   Feb 19, 1904
See Hackney, Miss Nora

RIDGELY, Miss Addie   Mar 14, 1901
See Wallace, Salem

RIDGELY, Charles W.   Local   Jul 31, 1903
Charles W. Ridgely, a son of E.W. Ridgely, of this village and Miss Mabel
Markham, were married at Quincy Monday. They came to Golden Tuesday to
visit few days with groom's parents. Mr Ridgely is employed as a' baker
at Bushnell where they will live.

RITTLER, Mrs Celia   Local   Sep 25, 1902
Mrs Celia Rittler, who formerly lived in Camp Point township, was married
in Quincy Tuesday to Chas. Upright, a poultry merchant.

ROBBINS, Miss Conie   Apr 5, 1896
See Orton, Daniel

ROBBINS, Miss Grace   Oct 31, 1902
See Alexander, P.L.

ROBBINS, James   Aug 18, 1898
See Worman, Miss Edna

ROBBINS, Miss Millie C.   Nov 7, 1901
See Burke, Chas. L.

ROBBINS, Miss Myrtle Blanche   Elm Grove   Mar 13, 1902
Miss Myrtle Blanche Robbins and Chas. Edgar Bagby of Red Oak, Texas were
quietly married at the parsonage of the Methodist Church at LaPrairie last
Wednesday eve by pastor Rev Hartwick and Friday eve left for home of
bridegroom in Texas.

ROBBINS, Mr and Mrs Nathan   Local   Oct 27, 1898
Mr and Mrs Nathan Robbins passed their 50th wedding anniversary, their
golden anniversary last Monday. Their children are all living and have
homes near them except one son in Oklahoma.

ROBERTS, Bruce   Mar 18, 1904
   See Davis, Miss Eva
ROBERTS, Frank   Bowen   Feb 22, 1896
   Married at he brides home, Thursday, February 20th in Houston, Miss Cora
   Smith, daughter of J.Q. Smith to Frank Roberts.
ROBERTS, Mrs Mattie   Camp Point   Jun 5, 1902
   Mr VanValen, of Missouri and Mrs Mattie Roberts, of this place, were mar-
   ried last Thursday eve.
ROBERTS, Dr R.B.   Local   Jun 12, 1902
   The marriage of Dr R.B. Roberts and Miss Bertha DeGroot, a niece of
   Supervisor W.H. DeGroot, is announced to take place today.
ROBERTSON, Chas.   Camp Point   Dec 22, 1898
   The marriage of Chas. Robertson and Miss Myrtle Boytz, both of Mendon will
   take place at high noon Wednesday at the home of Mr and Mrs Geo. Francis i
   Quincy. Grooms parents James and Mrs Robertson will give a 6 PM dinner
   to near relatives.
ROBERTSON, Miss Edith   Jun 10, 1904
   See Oliver, Harry
ROBERTSON, Miss Florence   Wedding   Feb 1, 1900
   Payson, Illinois January 26th Thursday, January 25th a quiet home wedding
   Miss Florence Robertson and John P. McGinnis were married at high noon.
   Wedding march was played by Mrs C.R. Morrison. Married by Rev Bonefon.
   Prayer was offered by C.R. Morrison, pastor of the bride. Miss Robertson
   is only daughter of Mr and Mrs John Robertson, is well known here and in
   Quincy, a graduate of Payson High School and also of the elocution depart-
   ment of Chaddock College. Mr McGinnis is a graduate of Chaddock College
   and has been studying for the ministry. He is a relative of Sam Woods, of
   Quincy. Rev Bonefon was a classmate of the groom and Miss McGinnis.
   " Quincy Whig"
ROBERTSON, Ralph   Mar 15, 1900
   See Willard, Miss Nellie
ROBINSON, Arch   Local   Aug 28, 1902
   Marriage of Arch Robinson and Miss Bertha Ramsey occurred at Bowen Sunday.
ROBINSON, Miss Lizzie   Jan 3, 1901
   See West, Tobe
ROSE, Miss Nellie   Camp Point   Oct 16, 1897
   Miss Nellie Rose, formerly of this village, was married in Chicago, on
   September 26th to Charles E. Hyde, a real estate man.
ROSENBOOM, Anton   May 16, 1896
   See Nebur, Miss Kate
ROSS, Miss Effie   Married   Mar 13, 1902
   LaPrairie, Illinois March 5th Married here tonight at the home of J.T. Ro
   their daughter, Miss Effie Ross and Walter Eyman by Rev Hartwick, pastor o
   ME Church. Wedding supper served. Will live LaPrairie. Guests were, Mr
   and Mrs E. Eyman, Mr and Mrs A.S. Robbins, Mr and Mrs D. Eyman, Mrs Jos.
   Cromwell, Mr and Mrs Archie Cummings of Louisiana, Missouri, Mr and Mrs
   W.W. Robbins, Mr and Mrs Eugene Ketchum, Mr and Mrs J.H. Robbins, Mrs
   Donelly, Mr and Mrs E.P. Carlin, Mr and Mrs Geo. White, Mr and Mrs E.H.
   Bacon, Lawrence Eyman, Clyde Eyman, Grace Robbins, Arthur Robbins and
   H. Pearce.
ROSS, Effie   LaPrairie   Mar 13, 1902
   Effie Ross and Walter Eyman were married at the home of brides parents,
   Mr and Mrs J.T. Ross, Wednesday eve, March 5th.
ROSSEN, Chester A.   Local   Nov 8, 1900
   Chester S. Rossen of Clayton and Clara M. Sells of Camp Point were license
   to wed Monday.

RUBY, Mabel   Jul 5, 1900
    See Blansett, Luther
RUDDELL, Miss Lottie Salome   Feb 5, 1904
    See Hartley, Rev D.H.
RUFLESON, Mr C.   Jan 9, 1902
    See Gooding, Miss Eliza
RUGGLES, Miss Beulah   Jun 28, 1900
    See Ferguson, F.E.
RULIFSON, Claude   Local   Jan 2, 1902
    Claude Rulifson, of West Union, Iowa and Miss Eliza Gooding, of Camp Point
    were married recently.
RUNYON, Charles   York Neck   Mar 19, 1898
    Supplement   Married at brides parents, Thursday eve, Charles Runyon and
    Annie Reece, both well known here.
RUSSELL, Harvey   Jan 18, 1896
    See Greenback, Mrs Tat
RUTLEDGE, Harley   Local   Jan 9, 1902
    Harley Rutledge and Miss Ethel McFarland, of Camp Point, were married Tuesday.
SAATHOFF, Miss Antka   Local   Mar 16, 1898
    Marriage license issued to John Garrelts, of Basco, and Miss Antka Saathoff,
    of Golden.
SAATHOFF, Miss Antka   Local   Mar 16, 1898
    John Garretts, of Basco, and Miss Antka Saathoff, of this place, were mar-
    ried Wednesday eve at the East Side German Church by Rev Oorrow. Both are
    popular young german people.
SAATHOFF, Miss Depka   Mar 14, 1896
    See Bartells, Bartell
SAATHOFF, Frank   Local   Nov 6, 1903
    A marriage license was issued Tuesday to Frank Saathoff, of Royal, Champaign
    County Illinois and Miss Lena Behrens, of Clayton.
SAATHOFF, Frank   Local   Nov 20, 1903
    Should have published last week: Marriage of Frank Saathoff, of Royal,
    Illinois and Miss Lena Behrens, of Clayton (bride is daughter of Harm
    Behrens) at the Prairie Chruch. They will live in Champaign County.
SAMMENDS, Miss Myrta   Feb 1, 1896
    See Rice, Geo. H.
SAMS, Miss Edna D.   Aug 5, 1904
    See Jones, J.C.
SARTORIUS, Miss Annie   Nov 30, 1899
    See Burmeister, John
SAWIN, Miss Kate   Oct 5, 1899
    See Castle, Joseph
SAWTELLE, Miss Jennie J.   Bowen   Apr 11, 1896
    Last Thursday eve April 7th at 8:30 PM at the home of Mrs Mary Sawtelle,
    occurred the marriage of her youngest daughter, Miss Jennie J. to Willaim
    J. Whitford, by Rev C.K. Westfall the former being born and raised in this
    city.
SAWTELLE, Miss Lillie   Bowen   Mar 28, 1896
    Married Sunday eve at 5 PM at the home of her mother, Miss Lillie Sawtelle
    to George Barker, of near Augusta by Rev C.K. Westfall.
SCEARCE, Emmett   Augusta   Oct 25, 1900
    Last Wednesday, at Plattsburg, Missouri occurred the marriage of Miss
    Gertrude Artz to Emmett Scearce. Bride was born and raised in our midst.
    She is daughter of Edwin Artz, deceased. She has made her home with her
    sister for past 2 years. Groom is assistant circuit clerk of his county.
    Will be at home at Plattsburg after November 1st.

SCHOENE, Miss Mary   Local   Mar 29, 1900
    Albert Post and Miss Mary Schoene, of this place were married last Friday
    afternoon at East Side Church by Rev Dorow.
SCHOENE, Oltman   Local   Nov 27, 1903
    Marriage license was issued this week to Oltman Schoene, of Golden and Miss
    Alice Buss, of Camp Point.
SCHOENEMAN, Eilert   Local   Sep 18, 1902
    At the home of Geo. H. Flesner Sunday eve a party was given in honor of
    Eilert Schoeneman and Miss Therisa Severins. It is reported the reported
    the young couple will be married on their return to the eastern part of
    the state.
SCHOENEMAN, Minnie and Miss Anna   Local   Oct 23, 1903
    Miss Anna Schoeneman left Monday for Champaign, where she attended the wedd
    of her sister, Minnie, which occurred Wednesday eve.
SCHONE, Miss Barbara   Local   Sep 8, 1905
    Jurgen J. Meints and Miss Barbara Schone both of South Prairie were mar-
    ried Thursday of last week.
SCHONE, George J.   Wedding   Feb 10, 1905
    George J. Schone and Ida J. Gronewold were married at Immanuel German
    Luther Church in Golden on Wednesday at 7 PM by Rev Ferd Alpers. Reception
    and supper at home of the bride following wedding. Groom is son of John
    B. Schone, of Shatten. Bride is daughter of Mr and Mrs John H. Gronewold,
    of LaPrairie. Will live on farm east of Chatten in near future.
SCHONE, Lina   Local   Feb 8, 1900
    Renke B. Lenerts, of Golden and Lina Schone, of Chatten, were licensed to
    wed last week.
SCHONE, Minnie   Chatten   Feb 27, 1902
    The marriage of Jasper Aden and Minnie Schone took place in Golden Sunday A
SCHONEMAN, Miss Eureka   Local   Sep 15, 1905
    Miss Eureka Schoneman, of Macomb and Mr I.B. Dace, of Rushville, Illinois
    were married at Rushville Sunday September 10th.
SCHRIVER, Frank   Fowler   Apr 8, 1898
    Married at the home of the bride, Frank Schriver and Miss Mattie Meyers,
    last week.
SCHROEDER, John M.L.   Dec 1, 1905
    See Guenther, Miss Lena Kate
SCHROEDER, Paul   Local   Dec 24, 1896
    Wonder is Paul Schroeder is married.
SCHROEDER, Paul   Married   Apr 5, 1900
    Paul Schroeder and Miss Maude M. Groves will be married at the home of
    brides parents in Plymouth, Illinois next Sunday at 6 PM. Bride elect
    is daughter of Mr and Mrs J.M. Groves highly respected Plymouth people.
    She is secretary of the Baptist Sunday School at that place. Mr Schroeder
    is son of L.C. Schroeder, of Camp Point township was for several years a
    solicitor for Quincy papers, working at different times for the Whig and
    Journal. He is now proprietor of the Occidental Hotel in Quincy.
    Will live Quincy.
SCHUESSLER, Clara Elizabeth and Henry F.   Oct 25, 1900
    Among divorce cases dismissed in circuit court this week was that of Clara
    Elizabeth Schuessler vs Henry F. Schuessler.
SCHUESSLER, Mrs Fred   Wants a Divorce   Jul 19, 1900
    Wife of Fred Schuessler, of this village, who left her husband about two we
    ago now asks for a divorce and charges her husband with repeated cruelty.
    Mr Schuessler says that the only semblance of trouble that he had with his
    wife was while he was attempting to prevent her from beating the children,
    of which there are seven.

SCHWANKE, C.F.   Aug 3, 1899
    See Worman, Miss Lou
SCHWANKE, Mrs Charles   LaPrairie   Sep 21, 1899
    Mrs Charles Schwanke, of Rockport, Illinois, lately married, returned
    Saturday to visit..
SCHWANKE, Miss Hannah   Dec 26, 1901
    See Gillepsie, Henry S.
SCHWARTZ, Dr Charles W.   Jul 28, 1898
    See Strickler, Miss Josephine
SCHWARTZ, Miss Mae   Local   Jul 11, 1901
    On Thursday, July 4th in the Judson Memorial Church of New York City, occurred
    the wedding of Miss Mae Schwartz, of this city, to Mr Benjamin L. Reitman,
    of Chicago. Before returning to their home in Chicago they will spend a
    few weeks abroad.
SCOTT, Oliver   Married   Nov 14, 1901
    At 6 PM today, Mr Oliver Scott, of Ambrose, and Miss Clara Walker, eldest
    daughter of James R. Walker and wife will be married at the home of brides
    parents 5½ miles south of Augusta. Miss Pearl Walker, sister of bride will
    play the wedding march and Rev J.H. Hartick of LaPrairie will pronounce
    them man and wife. Will go to housekeeping on the Bob Robison place ½ mile
    south of Ambrose.
SCOTT, Walter   York Neck   Mar 7, 1901
    Wednesday February 27th, occured the wedding of Walter Scott, of Mendon,
    to Miss Rathburn, of Quincy. Wedding took place in Quincy.
SEALOCK, C.R.   Local   Jun 3, 1904
    Cards received in this village telling of marriage of C.R. Sealock, of
    Golden, to Miss Mabel Fern Clark, of Eureka on May 28th. Mr and Mrs
    Sealock will be at home to friends in Golden after June 10th.
SEATON, Charles   Local   Jun 27, 1901
    Last evening at Chicago, Charles Seaton, of Golden, and Miss Elizabeth
    Virginia Wayman were married. Miss Maude Seaton attended the wedding.
SEATON, Charles Drake   Wedded   Jul 11, 1901
    Charles Drake Seaton, one of Golden's finest young men, and Miss Elizabeth
    V. Wayman, of Chicago were married in that city Wednesday June 26th by
    Rev Kindred, of the South Side Christian Church, Prof. G.T. Walker
    translated the service into the sign language of the contracting parties.
    John A. McIlvaine, a college chum of the grooms from Philadelphia was best
    man and Mrs J.B. Young sister of the bride, matron of Honor. Miss Pauline
    Acheson was bridesmaid and Mr W.B. Wayman, brother of bride was usher.
    After spending two weeks at Buffalo, Mr and Mrs Seaton will visit at Golden
    until September 1st when they will start housekeeping at Devil's Lake, ND.
    where the groom has a position as teacher in the state school for the deaf.
SEATON, Mr and Mrs Geo. K.   Local   Jan 12, 1899
    The Seaton case, wherein Mrs Geo. K. Seaton was sueing Mr Seaton for seperate
    maintainance has been compromized. Mr Seaton paying $1,500.00 and the costs
    of the case.
SEATON, Mrs Hester A. and George K.   Local   May 27, 1898
    Mrs Hester A. Seaton has sued her husband George K. Seaton, of this place
    for seperate maintainance and $500 attorney fees. The trouble between them
    arose over their children. Mrs Seaton is in Hancock County.
SEATON, Tom   Review   Feb 6, 1902
    December 2, 1893 Tom Seaton and Miss Laura Curry were wedded at Camp Point.

SEEHUSEN, Mr and Mrs John   Local   Aug 5, 1904
    Mr and Mrs John Seehusen have again decided that married life is misery.
    Tuesday they agreed to seperate and Mrs Seehusen took the train for
    Nebraska. John remains with us to spend his time in "single blessedness".
SEEHUSEN, John   Local   Apr 15, 1904
    At the grooms home in Golden Monday eve occurred the wedding of John Seehu
    and Mrs Mary Boettcher by Rev Dorrow. Bride recently came from Nebraska
    to meet Mr Seehusen, with matrimonial expectations. That they both were
    favorably impressed is proven by their wedding Monday.
SELBY, Miss Amnata   Dec 26, 1896
    See Sterrett, C.C.
SELBY, Miss Edna   Apr 24, 1897
    See Selby, Elmer T. (double marriage)
SELBY, Miss Electa   Mar 14, 1896
    See Beckett, John
SELBY, Miss Ellecta B.   Local   Mar 7, 1896
    Married at Camp Point, Wednesday eve March 4th, Miss Ellecta B. Selby to
    Jno. Beckett by Rev Dilley. Bride is daughter of H.E. Selby and wife. Th
    groom is son of Jos. Beckett, residing a few miles this side of Camp Point
SELBY, Elmer T.   Two Notable Weddings   Apr 24, 1897
    Elmer T. Selby, of this place and Miss Stella Huckelbury of Birmham, Iowa
    were married at Keokuk Thursday. Will probably live this city.
    At same hour married also were Earnest L. Moore and Miss Edna Selby,
    youngest daughter of townsman H.E. Selby were married. Mr Moore is in
    jewelry business. He is son of Warren Moore, who recently moved here from
    Huntsville. Miss Selby is a graduate of Golden high school in 96. Will
    live with Mr Moore's parents in this city.
SELBY, Ralph E.   Married in Kansas   Feb 19, 1898
    From a copy of the Walnut, Kansas Eagle, we learn of the marriage of Ralph
    E. Selby, to Miss Bessie G. Martin, January 20th. Mr Selby is son of Jas.
    Selby and wife who resided here up to about two years ago. The infare
    was held at the superb home of Mr and Mrs James Selby on Friday.
SELBY, Miss Urith   Dec 20, 1902
    See Joslin, Bertrice E.
SELIGSOHN, Mr Leo   Mar 24, 1905
    See Aull, Miss E. Blanche
SELLS, Clara M.   Nov 8, 1900
    See Rossen, Chester A.
SEVERINS, Miss Therisa   Sep 18, 1902
    See Schoeneman, Eilert
SEXTON, Wm   Historical   Apr 18, 1901
    March 25, 1893 Wm Sexton and Blanche Sellers were married.
SEYLER, Lewis C.   Oct 6, 1905
    See Walker, Pearl
SHAKE, Marvin A.   Local   Jan 18, 1900
    Last Monday Marvin A. Shake and Miss Nora Asher, both of Coatsburg, were
    licensed to be married.
SHAKE, William J.   Local   Nov 20, 1903
    Marriage license issued Monday to William J. Shake, of Camp Point, and
    Miss Clara Gibbs, of Coatsburg.
SHARP, Amos   Camp Point   Jan 22, 1898
    Amos Sharp of Clayton and Miss Lizzie Hocamp of this place, went to Quincy
    Wednesday and were married.
SHAY, James   Local   May 1, 1902
    James Shay, of Big Neck, and Miss Edna Haistings, of Mendon, were married
    last week.

SHELEY, Walter   Camp Point   Sep 25, 1897
    Walter Sheley, of Bushnell, and Miss Lottie Bartells will be married at
    the brides home Wednesday eve of this week.
SHELLY, Mr   Pea Ridge   May 1, 1897
    Mr Shelly, of Mounds, and Miss Ella May, daughter of Mr and Mrs Thomas May
    were married at the home of the bride, near Shank's Sunday night a week ago.
SHEPHERD, Mr and Mrs   Chili   Feb 21, 1901
    Mr and Mrs James Norris attended the silver wedding of Mr and Mrs Shepherd,
    of Carthgae last Saturday February 9th.
SHEPHERD, Miss Vina   Oct 10, 1896
    See Lambert, Mr
SHEPHERD, William   Aug 28, 1902
    See Kindhart, Miss Hannah
SHERRICK, Darrah Luther   Aug 22, 1901
    See Owen, Miss Ella
SHERRICK, Mr Luther   Aug 22, 1901
    See Owen, Miss Ella
SHERRICK, Miss Susie   Aug 30, 1900
    See Byrones, Archibal
SHONE, Miss Christina   Feb 8, 1896
    See Aden, Ranke H.
SHRADER, Miss Jennie   Aug 24, 1899
    See Groves, Daniel R.
SHRADER, Jós..O..   Jan 6, 1905
    See Taylor, Miss Jennie
SHRIVER, James   York Neck   Feb 23, 1899
    James Shriver and Miss Lutrecia Cubbage were married last Wednesday at home
    of brides parents.
SHRIVER, James   Feb 23, 1899
    See Cubbage, Theresa
SHROAT, Bartlett   Married   Dec 20, 1900
    At the home of officiating minister, Rev Shaffer, at Hermon, Illinois, on
    Sunday December 9th, Bartlett Shroat and Miss Pearl Barnes were united in
    marriage. Only a few relatives and friends attended, after which they
    attended church and repaired to home of brides parents for a sumptuous
    dinner. Bride is daughter of a prosperous Knox County farmer. Groom
    came here from Louisville, Kentucky some four years ago and spent three
    years in Adams County where he will be remembered by many friends.
SIEBERT, Matthew M.   Local   Jun 14, 1900
    Marriage license was issued Monday to Matthew M. Siebert of Galesburg and
    Miss Margaret E. Davis, of Camp Point.
SIEGAL, John   Fairview   Nov 7, 1901
    John Siegel, of Fairview and Miss Nora Wilhite, of Bowen were married last
    Wednesday eve in the home of brides mother.
SIEPER, John   Weyerts, Nebraska   May 29, 1897
    Last Sunday occurred the marriage of John Sieper and Pada Fierichs at the
    home of the brides father, Harm Fierichs.
SIMMONDS, Sam and wife   Camp Point   Mar 8, 1900
    Last Tuesday was the 10th wedding anniversary of Sam Simmonds and wife.
SIMMONS, Jas. W.   Local   Jul 10, 1902
    Jas. W. Simmons, of Owassa, Michigan and Miss Ella M. Grubb, of Liberty,
    were married last week. Miss Grubb was at one time Supt. of schools of
    Adams County. She also taught at Camp Point for a number of years.
SIMON, Miss Emma   Jan 3, 1901
    See Webster, Ernest

SIMPSON, Jasper L.   Elm Grove   Jan 13, 1905
   Jasper L. Simpson, of Augusta, and Miss Adora Underwood, of Elm Grove were
   married in Quincy Thursday by Judge McCrory.
SLAGLE, Miss   LaPrairie   Mar 23, 1899
   Miss Cora Mathes returned Monday from Clayton, where she attended the wedd-
   of Miss Slagle.
SLATER, James and Jennie   Miserable Married Men   Jul 4, 1896
   Divorce case of James Slater vs Jennie Slater, husband is now at Soldiers
   Home. They were married LaGrange in 1882 and wife left him in 1885 and wen
   to live on Bay Island and then Long Island. She is now in LaGrange, Mis-
   souri her earlier home.
SLIGARD, Mr   Aug 19, 1904
   See Miller, Widow
SLOANE, Mrs Maggie   Local   Jun 15, 1899
   Mrs Maggie Sloane, age 22, a married lady with two children was adjuded
   insane in county court Monday and taken to Jacksonville.
SMITH, Clara R.   Oct 24, 1901
   See Rhea, Robert C.
SMITH, Clyde M.   Exchanges   Sep 8, 1905
   Mr Clyde M. Smith, of Bowen and Miss Elzie M. Veach, of Clayton, were mar-
   ried at Quincy last Wednesday by Rev A.K. Byrns of Bowen.
SMITH, Miss Cora   Feb 22, 1896
   See Roberts, Frank
SMITH, Miss Emma   May 15, 1897
   See Adams, Prof, W.T.
SMITH, Geo.   Local   Feb 20, 1902
   Geo. Smith, of Coatsburg and Susie Warren, of Camp Point, were married
   last week.
SMITH, Ira D.   Local   May 20, 1904
   Marriage license issued Tuesday to Ira D. Smith, of Bowen, and Miss Mary F.
   Thompson, of same village.
SMITH, Leafie   Married   Jun 24, 1904
   On Wednesday eve of last week at the home of Mr and Mrs John Q. Smith, 6½
   miles southwest of Bowen occurred the wedding of their daughter, Leafie,
   to Edwin Owens at 8 PM by Rev A.K. Burns of Bowen. Bride attended by Miss
   Bernice Gorby and groom by Hurley Smith, a brother of bride. Will go to
   housekeeping at once.
SMITH, Miss Lizzie   May 2, 1901
   See Mayson, Andy
SMITH, Ruth   Tales of Pioneers   Mar 16, 1899
   Following account is of a wedding in Mound township in primitive times of
   the early settlers of the county and is from the Bordolph News. It appears
   that the news was wrong in stating that the marriage of Edward Dryer was
   first solemnized in Mound township. T.J. Creel tells us that a wedding
   occured prior to that time about 1836 in which one Osborn and a lady named
   Ruth Smith, who lived in a cabin somewhere between the present dwellings
   of G.A. Singer and R.C. Wilcox. Mr Creel was a boy at the time, but his
   father and mother attended the wedding. It occurred before breakfast, afte
   ceremony the bride and groom walked to Pennington Point for the infair
   because they had no vehicles. Miss Ruth made the ten mile walk with out
   shoes as she had borrowed a pair for the wedding.
SMITH, Miss Sadie L.   Nov 6, 1903
   See Goodnow, Fred H.
SMITH, Wilson   Dec 22, 1898
   See Eaton, Miss Dora

SMURR, Miss Mabel   Nov 25, 1904
    See Downing, James
SNIDER, Emma   May 22, 1897
    See Pope, Lenard
SPARKS, Curtis   Married at Bentley   Jan 23, 1903
    Marriage of Mr Curtis Sparks to Miss Ida Powell occurred at the home of
    Frank Powell, near Bentley, Wednesday January 14th. Mr Sparks is son of
    Mr and Mrs T.J. Sparks and is a successful teacher. Miss Powell is a sister
    of Mr Geo. Powell and grew to womanhood near Bowen. "Bowen Chronicle"
SPEARS, John   Local   Dec 25, 1903
    On Tuesday Fred Stewart and wife went to Perry, Illinois where they attended
    on Thursday the wedding of Mrs Stewarts brother, John Spears, and Miss
    Margaret Dorsey. Groom is a traveling salesman for a Quincy firm.
SPEARS, Miss Kathryn   Home Wedding   Sep 25, 1902
    From Ursa Times: On Wednesday eve, September 17th, 1902 at the home of
    brides parents, Mr and Mrs Abe Spears, occurred the wedding of their dau-
    ghter, Kathryn to Mr Alfred P. Stewart, of Golden, by Rev S.N. Wakefield
    of Mendon at 6:30 PM. Wedding march played by Mr Willard Stewart, brother
    of groom. Bride born and raised near Ursa. Groom is second son of W.S.
    Stewart of Golden, a well to do stock dealer. Those from a distance
    were: Mr and Mrs W.S. Stewart and family, Mr and Mrs Charles Poling, all
    of Golden, Mr and Mrs R.I. Burrows and daughter, Fern of Quincy, Miss
    Flossie Egley, of Quincy.
SPEARS, Miss Kathryn   Sep 18, 1902
    See Stewart, Fred
STAHL, Miss Edith   Aug 28, 1897
    See Henry, Dr E.C.
STAHL, John M.   Married in Chicago   Jun 28, 1900
    John M. Stahl and Miss Mamie C. Choteau Platt, daughter of Mr and Mrs Henry
    S. Platt, of 4046 Prairie Ave, Chicago were married at Grace Episcopal
    Church, Chicago last Monday at 8 PM by Rev Ernest M. Stires. Miss Bessie
    M. Emmart, of Englewood, was maid of honor, bridesmaids were, Miss Marion
    E. Philips, of Laporte, Indiana, Miss Zoe Baylis of Springfield, Illinois
    Miss Grace L. Sterling and Miss L. Eleanor Oliver of Chicago. Joseph M.
    Hirons was best man and S. Choteau Platt, Otto Dorner, of Milwaukee, M.T.
    Moss and W. Hobart Emmart acted as ushers. Reception in birdes home.
    Will live at 4328 Langely Ave Chicago after September 10th. Mt Stahl
    was reared on a farm in Houston township and has done well as an agricul-
    tural writer and publisher of farming periodicals.
STAMBAUGH, Miss   Apr 10, 1897
    See Champ, Mr
STANLEY, Wm   Local   Sep 25, 1897
    Wm Stanley and Miss Effie Hedrick, of Augusta, were married in Keokuk Monday
    the bride and groom are cousins and for five years trying to get consent
    of their parents to marry. Recently it was secured and as Illinois law
    forbids marriages between cousins, they went to Iowa to be married.
STARK, C.H.   Augusta   Jan 3, 1901
    C.H. Stark, of this place, and Miss Ola Boman, of Plymouth, were married
    at the home of Rev Hall, in that city, last Sunday eve. Groom was born
    and raised here. He is son of J.W. Stark and wife. Will live on his
    fathers farm near Greensburg, Missouri.
STATES, Miss Inez G.   May 6, 1904
    See McMurray, J. Logan
STEED, Prof A.   Pine Grove   Mar 8, 1900
    It is reported that Prof A. Steed formerly of this place, but now of Newport
    Rhose Island was married last week.

STEED, Miss Elizabeth   Nov 14, 1896
    See Paxton, Hayes
STEELE, Chas.   LaPrairie   Mar 29, 1900
    Mr Chas. Steele and Miss Fannie Winfield were married in Quincy Tuesday las
    Will occupy the Hughes property.
STEELE, Miss Frankie   LaPrairie   Jul 1, 1904
    Miss Grace Pearce, Harold and Mary Hogsett attended wedding of Miss Frankie
    Steele at Galesburg Wednesday.
STEINBRECHER. Henry   Local   Jan 30, 1902
    Henry Steinbrecher and Miss Pearl Todd were married last Thursday at the
    home of the brides parents in York Neck.
STEINBRECHER, Miss Rosa   Dec 26, 1901
    See Todd, Wm L. Jr.
STEINERT, Albert   Jun 10, 1904
    See McMullen, Miss Ida
STENHERNBURG, Miss Della   Primrose   Feb 8, 1896
    Miss Della Stenhernburg of Primrose and Fred Brier of Camp Point were mar-
    ried Thursday. Will live near West Point where Mr Brier owns a farm.
STERRETT, C.C.   5 Years Ago   Dec 26, 1896
    C.C. Sterrett, of Bowen and Miss Ammata Selby were married in this city.
STEVENS, Miss Catherine   Jul 12, 1900
    See Dutton, Prof. Frank F.
STEVENS, Miss Lena   Weyerts, Nebraska   Mar 9, 1899
    Miss Lena Stevens was to have been married at Gothenburg last week but she
    took the measles and the ceremony was postponed.
STEVENS, Miss Mary   Henry, Nebraska   Mar 14, 1901
    Miss Mary Stevens and Carl Tharel were married March 6th.
STEWART, Alfred P.   Sep 25, 1902
    See Spears, Miss Kathryn
STEWART, Fred   Local   Sep 18, 1902
    Fred Stewart, of this village, and Miss Kathryn Spears, of Ursa, were mar-
    ried at the home of the brides parents yesterday.
STEWART, Miss Grace E.   Apr 10, 1897
    See Poling, Chas.
STEWART, Mark   Wedding   Oct 21, 1904
    On Thursday at 3 PM at the ME parsonage, occurred the wedding of Mr Mark
    Stewart to Miss Daisy Thomas, of Huntsville. Illinois. Mr Stewart is a
    painter by trade. Miss Thomas while a stranger to the most of us is a
    Christian lady. Will live Houston township.
STIERENBURG, Lina   Nov 9, 1899
    See Fink, Andreas H.
STIFFY, Miss Susan   Clayton   Jan 1, 1898
    Wedding at home of John Stiffy Christmas Day. Miss Susan Stiffy, of this
    place, and a Mr Cronin of Decatur, Illinois by Rev A.H. Sears.
STILWELL, Miss Lottie   Dec 4, 1897
    See Morris, Orvil
STINSON, C.W.   Review   Jan 30, 1902
    November 18, 1893 C.W. Stinson and Miss Della Beckett were married.
STOESZEL, Miss Lizzie   Mar 13, 1897
    See Fingerhim, Gotleb
STOVER, Frederick   Horeb   Feb 17, 1905
    Frederick Stover, of Pine Grove and Miss Lizzie Houck, of Augusta slipped
    away from their friends Monday and went to Macomb where they were married.
    They are visiting the grooms parents, Mr and Mrs Joseph Stover, of near
    Pine Grove at present.

STOVER, Wm   Feb 28, 1901
   See Dutton, Miss Bertie
STRICKLER,   Local   Oct 6, 1905
   Mrs Ollie Eckles, of Skidmore, Missouri was here this week to attend the
   Strickler, Graham wedding.
STRICKLER, Jeremiah   Historical   Apr 25, 1901
   April 15, 1893 Jeremiah Strickler and Miss Laura Ralph were married..
STRICKLER, Joe   Local   Oct 6, 1905
   Joe Strickler and Miss Grace Graham were married at the brides home near
   Bowen at 7:30 PM Wednesday October 4th. Will live on the Wilbur Strickler
   farm west of Golden.
STRICKLER, Joseph   Oct 13, 1905
   See Graham, Grace
STRICKLER, Miss Josephine   Wedding   Jul 28, 1898
   "Topeka, Kansas Journal" Married Wednesday eve, Miss Josephine Strickler
   and Dr Charles W. Schwartz of Quincy, Illinois at the brides home on Quincy
   Street. Bridal party led by Miss Enid Strickler and Master Lucien
   Strickler, Miss Mary Huron was bridesmaid. Mrs L.H. Strickler sang a solo.
   Ceremony by Dr Countermine and Dr Embree. Will live Camp Point.
STRICKLER, Miss Josie   Jul 21, 1898
   See Schwartz, Dr C.W.
STUBBENS, Miss Margaret   Mar 31, 1905
   See Doren, Harm
STUBBINS, Fred and wife   8 Years Ago   Aug 1, 1901
   June 24, 1893   Fred Stubbins and wife celebrated their 25th wedding
   anniversary.
STUBBINS, Miss Lena   Feb 24, 1905
   See Beinhoff, Harm
STUHRENBERG, Henry   Local   Dec 23, 1904
   Henry Stuhrenberg.and Miss Josie Baker were quietly married at Carthage
   last week.
STUMP, Roy   Big Neck   Nov 4, 1904
   Roy Stump,-of Big Neck, and Miss Nancy Hughlett, of Plymouth were married
   at Quincy Wednesday October 26th by Rev Parker Shields.
STUMP, Violet   Apr 12, 1900
   See Hudson, Orves
SUDDETT, Miss Lillie   Dec 26, 1896
   See Hail, Mr
SUTER, Miss Osa   Apr 10, 1903
   See Bennett, Freddie
SUTER, Miss Stella   May 1, 1903
   See Gates, Oliver
SUTHERLAND, Nellie   Fairview   Dec 4, 1903
   Wm Sutherland and family attended wedding of Nellie Sutherland and Mr Tuttle
   at the home of Dr Sutherland near Stillwell last Sunday eve.
SUTHERLAND, Nellie   Bethel   Dec 4, 1903
   Andrew Ketchum and wife spent Sunday with Dr Sutherland of Woodville, and
   attended the wedding of their daughter Nellie to a Mr Tuttle.
SWAIN, Miss Effie   Feb 26, 1904
   See Nichols, Bert
SWAIN, Mary   Dec 20, 1902
   See Randles, Lawrence A.
SWANEY, Miss Grace Agnes   Jun 17, 1904
   See Black, Clarence
SWEIKERT, Wm   Local   Oct 17, 1901
   Marriage license was issued last week to Wm Sweikert, of Loraine and Miss
   Clara LaRonte, of Camp Point township.

SWISHER, Bert   Local   Jan 30, 1903
   Bert Swisher, of Bowen and Miss Jennie McClain, of LaPrairie, were married
   at Mt'Sterling last week. Will live near Bowen.
SYCKLE, George E.   Local   Aug 7, 1903
   George E. Syckle of Kellerville, and Miss Lulu Hobbs, of Clayton, were
   married recently. Bride was 15 years old.
SYLVESTER, Miss Flora   Dec 29, 1905
   See Coats, Paul
TALBOT, Mr and Mrs B.F.   Tin Wedding   Jun 13, 1896
   Wednesday eve June 10th being the 10th anniversary of the marriage of Mr
   and Mrs B.F. Talbot.
TANDY, Mr and Mrs H.L.   Local   Aug 19, 1904
   Mr and Mrs R.A. Beckett and family of Deerfield, Kansas arrived last week.
   They came to celebrate the golden wedding of Mr and Mrs H.L. Tandy, Mrs
   Becketts parents, of Newton and will spend a few days with relatives here.
TARR, Edna A.   Aug 28, 1903
   See Bunnels, Walter F.
TAYLOR, Miss Daisy E.   Jun 17, 1904
   See Ward, Foster M.
TAYLOR, Miss Jennie   Married   Jan 6, 1905
   Wednesday eve, January 4th at the home of the bride, occurred the marriage
   Miss Jennie Taylor, of Camp Point to Jos. O. Shrader, of East St Louis by
   Rev Leo. Howard at 5:30 PM. "O Promise Me" was sung by Miss Ethel Taylor.
   Bridal march was played by Miss Alice Taylor. Flower girl was Erma Black
   cousin of the bride and will live East St Louis after February 1st.
TAYLOR, Miss Lizzie E.   Nov 17, 1898
   See Grimes, Dr J.M.
TAYLOR, Mr and Mrs Scott   Local   Oct 13, 1898
   Mr and Mrs Scott Taylor reminded each other last Saturday that the day was
   their 20th wedding anniversary.
TAYLOR, Tom   Camp Point   Aug 29, 1896
   Tom Taylor and Mary Wishart were married recently.
TECHT, William M.   Local   Feb 23, 1899
   Marriage license has been issued to William M. Techt, of Basco and Miss
   Jennie Albers, of LaPrairie.
THANSMIDT, Fred   Camp Point   Dec 22, 1898
   Misses Myrtle Callahan and Julia Lawless attended the wedding of Fred
   Thansmidt and Anna Lawless at high noon Wednesday at the brides home
   near Columbus.
THAREL, Carl   Mar 14, 1901
   See Stevens, Miss Mary
THOMAS, Miss   Mar 24, 1894
   See Witt, Samuel
THOMAS, Miss   Review   Jun 12, 1902
   See Witt, Samuel
THOMAS, Miss Daisy   Oct 21, 1904
   See Stewart, Mark
THOMAS, Joseph L.   Wedding   Nov 21, 1901
   At the home of brides parents last Thursday eve at 6:30 Joseph L. Thomas,
   of Quincy and Miss Mattie E. Gans, of this village were married by Rev
   Wehrman. Left same evening for Quincy where they will live and where the
   groom as a good position as a school teacher which he has had for several
   terms. Bride taught school in Golden for a few years.
THOMAS, Walter   Local   Jun 5, 1902
   Walter Thomas and Miss Nina Morley, of Camp Point, were married last week.

THOMPSON, Miss Abbey   May 29, 1902
   See Bottorff, Otis
THOMPSON, Art   Oct 20, 1905
   See Thompson, Stella Mae
THOMPSON, Arthur   Local   Jan 25, 1900
   A couple from Big Neck, Arthur Thompson and Miss May Denny, came to town
   yesterday, and after considering the matter for a few hours, marched into
   Judge Heckenkamp's office and were married on the spot. Tuesdays Whig
THOMPSON, Miss Cora M.   Oct 27, 1905
   See Arnold, Otho M.
THOMPSON, Miss Dora   Aug 28, 1897
   See Butler, Mr C.F.
THOMPSON, Miss Dora   Aug 28, 1897
   See Butler, Frank
THOMPSON, George   Henry, Nebraska   Feb 6, 1902
   Married recently, George Thompson and Miss Mary Jurgens.
THOMPSON, James   Elm Grove   Feb 22, 1896
   James Thompson and wife will make their newly married home on the Ackley
   farm.
THOMPSON, Miss Jessie   Dec 6, 1900
   See Ketchum, Vivian
THOMPSON, Miss Lizzie   Feb 6, 1902
   See Miller, George
THOMPSON, Miss Mary F.   May 20, 1904
   See Smith, Ira D.
THOMPSON, Miss Minnie   Oct 16, 1897
   See DeJean, C.B.
THOMPSON, Stella Mae   Fairview   Oct 20, 1905
   Married at residence of Lew Thompson, their daughter, Stella Mae to Art
   Thompson. Wedding march played by Miss Pearl Willard a close friend of
   bride. Ceremony performed by Rev Bert Taylor. Miss Stella is the
   youngest daughter of Lewis Thompson.
THOMPSON, William   Local   Dec 4, 1903
   William Thompson of Camp Point and Miss May Koetzle, of Quincy were married
   at Camp Point, Thursday of last week.
THOMPSON, Wm O.   Local   Mar 5, 1904
   A marriage license issued last week to Wm O. Thompson, of Bowen, and Miss
   Mary Boyd, of the same village.
TOACH, Miss Katie   Jan 23, 1902
   See Knight, Charley
TODD, Wm L. Jr.   Local   Dec 26, 1901
   Wm L. Todd Jr and Miss Rosa Steinbrecher, of York Neck neighborhood, were
   married last week.
TOTSCH, Albert   German Center   Apr 24, 1897
   Wednesday occurred the marriage of Albert Totsch and Miss Rika Behrens.
   Mr Totsch is second oldest son of Jacob Totsch. Miss Behrens is oldest
   daughter of Herman Behrens and wife. Married by Rev Oetting.
TRIBUNE, Miss Lucy   Camp Point   Jun 20, 1901
   Wedding of Miss Lucy Tribune and Charlie Ferrick is set for Wednesday of
   this week.
TROUT, Miss Nina   Dec 4, 1903
   See Eber, Alfred L.

TUGGLE, Thomas   Married in Jail   Jul 5, 1900
    Married in the cell room in McDonough County jail, Wednesday eve, June 20th
    Thomas Tuggle, under indictment for burglary and Miss Della Coddington, of
    the city by Justice W.G. McClellan in presence of the family of the groom
    and sheriff's family. Bride went to home of grooms parents, 337 N. Ward
    Street, where she still remains, Tom is 18 years old. Bride came to
    Macomb last fall from Kewanee and both were employed in a hotel. Miss
    Coddington before living at Kewanee lived at Princeton where she is said
    to own property. Her home originally was in Mendota. "Macomb By Stander"
TURNER, Miss Etta   Oct 6, 1894   Sep 18, 1902
    See Geibert, John
TURNER, Lawrence E.   Apr 22, 1904
    See LaRonte, Miss M. Lena
TURNER, Miss Zephy   Sep 23, 1904
    See Wysong, Hebert
TUTTLE, Mr   Dec 4, 1903
    See Sutherland, Nellie
TUXFORD, Miss Leona   Dec 12, 1901
    See Hudson, Huse
TYLER, Miss Myrtie   Bowen   Apr 11, 1896
    Married, Sunday, April 5th at high noon at the home of Mr and Mrs J.C. Tyler
    of this place, their daughter, Miss Myrtie, to W.W. Glaze of Versailles.
UNDERWOOD, Miss Adora   Jan 13, 1905
    See Simpson, Jasper L.
UNDERWOOD, George   Eloped   Oct 13, 1898
    Last Wednesday night George Underwood and Miss Pearl Alexander, who reside
    in Elm Grove neighborhood eloped. Taking with them a horse and buggy.
    George is 18 years old and girl but 14 years old, father and mother of
    girl is Mr and Mrs Daniel Alexander. Boy is son of Thos. Underwood.
    Later: Since writing the above the couple have returned and we under-
    stand they say they were married in Michigan. They are living at
    Underwoods.
UNDERWOOD, George   Married Again   Oct 20, 1898
    As George Underwood and Miss Pearl Alexander failed to secure a marriage
    certificate from the justice who married them, they procurred a license
    and were again married this week, this time in Quincy. They claim to have
    been married in the center of the Mississippi River by neglected to secure
    a certificate from the justice.
UNDERWOOD, George   Kidnapping Case   May 30, 1901
    Several years ago the social structure of Elm Grove was shaken by the elope-
    ment of George Underwood and Pearl Alexander. The girl was but 14 years o
    and boy slightly her senior. Girls parents never became reconciled to the
    marriage and lately quarrels arose between Underwood and wife and about tw
    weeks ago they seperated, the mother retaining possission of their two chi
    contrary to the wishes of the husband. Last Monday Mrs Underwood went in
    town with the oldest child who is about 2 years old. While in Boger's sto
    Underwood came and took the child out and down the street. Mother followe
    but was rebuffed by Underwood. Underwood arrested.
UNDERWOOD, George   Local   Sep 4, 1903
    George Underwood has sued his wife's parents, Daniel Alexander and Rachel
    Alexander, for $10,000 damages, claiming that they have prevented his wife
    from living with him.
UPCHURCH, Miss Grace   Aug 23, 1900
    See Yackle, Edd

UPRIGHT, Chas.   Sep 25, 1902
  See Rittler, Mrs Celia
UTESCH, Rev John H.   Local   May 27, 1904
  Invitations are out for wedding of Rev John H. Utesch and Miss Avina V.
  Eigenberg to take place in the German Lutheran Immanuels Church on Wednes-
  day eve June 1st.
UTESCH, Rev John H.   Married   Jun 3, 1904
  At the West Side German Lutheran Church Wednesday eve at 8 occurred the
  marriage of Rev John H. Utesch and Miss Alvina V. Eigenberg by Rev Alpers.
  Grooms home has been at Yutan, Nebraska. For several years he studied for
  the ministry at the Western Theological Seminary, Atchinson, Kansas where
  he recently graduated and just accepted his first charge as pastor of English
  Lutheran Church at Liberty, Illinois where they will live. Bride is daughter
  of Mr and Mrs John Eigenberg of this village and she took a course in
  music at Midland College, Atchison, Kansas. He will preach his first
  sermon at Liberty on June 5th.
VANBRUNT, Miss Clara   February 4, 1893   Jan 31, 1901
  See Crossland, Jacob
VANHORN, Eugene   Augusta   Apr 18, 1901
  Eugene VanHorn and Effie Pratt were married Sunday eve at Galesburg, where
  they will probably reside.
VANVALEN, Mr   Jun 5, 1902
  See Roberts, Mrs Mattie
VAUGHEN, Clifford W.   Aug 8, 1901
  See Witt, Adelia A.
VEACH, Miss Elzie M.   Sep 8, 1905
  See Smith, Clyde M.
VOLLBRACHT, Miss Emma   Jan 5, 1899
  See Hanke, John
VOLLROTH, Miss Minnie   Oct 13, 1898
  See Isense, Oscar
WADE, Miss Lennie   Nov 23, 1895
  See Barger, D. Austin
WALKER, A.J.   LaPrairie   Sep 6, 1900
  A.J. Walker, of this place was married to Mrs Mary Jane Moore, also of this
  place on Tuesday of last week at Mt Sterling. Will live LaPrairie.
WALKER, Miss Alma D.   Jan 20, 1905
  See Peck, Royal T.
WALKER, Miss Carrie   Sep 1, 1898
  See Alexander, William
WALKER, Chas.   Elm Grove   Jan 16, 1903
  Chas. Walker, son of Mr and Mrs C.W. Walker, and Miss Pearl Hedrick, of
  LaPrairie, went on the fast mail Wednesday to Quincy and were married there
  and returned on the first evening passenger.
WALKER, Miss Clara   Nov 14, 1901
  See Scott, Oliver
WALKER, Jesse   8 Years Ago   Oct 17, 1901
  August 12, 1893 Jesse Walker and Miss Mary Whitehead were married.
WALKER, Pearl   Wedding at Alma, Nebr.   Oct 6, 1905
  On Wednesday at 5 PM September 27th at the home of the brides parents Mr
  and Mrs James R. Walker, occurred the marriage of their daughter, Pearl to
  Mr Lewis C. Seyler to the strains of Lohengrins Bridal chorus played by
  sister of the groom, Miss Tina Seyler. Grooms father, Rev Theo Seyler,
  pronounced the words that made them man and wife.

WALLACE, Mr and Mrs A.R.   Golden Wedding   Jan 2, 1903
    Mr and Mrs A.R. Wallace celebrated their golden wedding Wednesday at their
    home in Camp Point township. They were married Dec 31, 1852. They are
    among the oldest residents of Adams County. Mr Wallace came to this county
    with his mother in 1831, when a boy of a dozen years and has lived on the
    same farm in Camp Point ever since. "Whig"
WALLACE, Mr and Mrs A.R.   Golden Wedding   Jan 9, 1903
    The 50th wedding anniversary of Mr and Mrs A.R. Wallace of Camp Point town-
    ship was celebrated at their beautiful home on Wednesday December 31st with
    about 40 friends. 1859-1902
WALLACE, Chas.   Married   Dec 19, 1896
    Married, Wednesday at high noon, two of Goldens young people, Chas. Wallace
    and Miss Irene McHatton in Quincy in presence of Mrs Cora McHatton of Camp
    Point and Miss Jennie Wallace and John McGinnis, of this place by Rev H.A.
    Ott, pastor of Luther Memorial Church. Groom is son of Mr and Mrs Jas. A.
    Wallace. Bride is daughter of R.G. McHatton and wife. Will live on a farm
    near Golden.
WALLACE, Miss Emma   Sep 1, 1898
    See Cunningham, Fred
WALLACE, John   Jul 8, 1898
    See Frazier, Miss Ada
WALLACE, John M.   Jul 1, 1898
    See Frazer, Miss Ada
WALLACE, Miss Lou   5 Years Ago   Oct 16, 1897
    See Carlin, Tom
WALLACE, Miss Mayme   Dec 26, 1896
    See McCray, Robert J.
WALLACE, Richard A.   Local   Jun 16, 1905
    Camp Point Journal says that Richard A. Wallace, of Los Angeles, California
    and Miss Lydia King were married at Los Angeles June 6th. Mr Wallace was
    formerly a banker at Camp Point.
WALLACE, Salem   Local   Mar 7, 1901
    Salem Wallace and Miss Addie Ridgely, two of Goldens finest young people,
    were wedded at Mt Sterling yesterday.
WALLACE, Salem   Matrimonial   Mar 14, 1901
    At the home of Mrs White Washburn in Mt Sterling on Wednesday of last week
    Salem Wallace and Miss Addie Ridgely of this place were married by Rev
    Eakins, of Mt Sterling Presbyterian Church. Will live in the Bartell
    property in west part of town.
WALTER, Chas. W.   Dec 22, 1905
    See Busboom, Miss Dorothy
WARD, Miss Eva   Sep 19, 1901
    See Wright, Walter
WARD, Foster M.   Wedding   Jun 17, 1904
    On Wednesday at 8 PM occurred the wedding of Foster M. Ward to Miss Daisy
    Taylor by Rev Hartley in the presence of relatives at the brides parents,
    Mr and Mrs John Taylor. Mr Ward whose home is in Winslow, Arizona is at
    present employed as a conductor on one of the Western R.R. lines. Will
    live Arizonia.
WARD, John Omer   Local   Jun 5, 1903
    John Omer Ward, of Camp Point and Miss Lottie Beckett, who is sweet
    seventeen and daughter of Rezin Beckett living south of Golden, were
    married at Camp Point Thursday of last week. Will live Camp Point.
WARD, Otho   Camp Point   Jan 30, 1902
    Otho Ward and Miss Jennie Dwire were married Sunday night at the home of
    Rev Cain.

WARD, Walter S.   Camp Point   Oct 20, 1898
    Married, Walter S. Ward and <u>Mrs</u> Lina Beal at Springfield.
WARREN, Susie   Feb 20, 1902
    See Smith. Geo.
WARTICK, Miss Emma   Jun 12, 1902
    See Sloan, William
WARTICK, John W.   Kansas News   Jun 26, 1903
    Clipped from May 27th issue of Wellington, Kansas newspaper: Married on
    Wednesday 4 PM May 20th at the home of Elder J.M. Via, this city, Mr John
    W. Wartick a prosperous farmer of near Portland, and Miss Myrtle, daughter
    of D.J. Ramsey of near Dalton, this county. Miss Etta Wartick, sister of
    the groom and Messrs John and Ulman Ramsey, brothers of the bride were in
    attendence.
WARTICK, Miss Mary   Oct 9, 1897
    See Marshall, Leileber
WARTICK, Miss Rosa   Jul 31, 1902
    See Miller, Oscar
WATSON, Elmer A.   Local   Dec 23, 1904
    Elmer A. Watson, one of Clayton's young business men, and <u>Mrs</u> Lulu B. Ausmus
    were married at the brides home in Clayton Sunday at 6 PM.
WATSON, John   Local   Apr 20, 1899
    John Watson, at one time a resident of Adams County, but now of Lawson,
    Missouri was guest of James A. Beckett and family this week. Mr Watson
    during the civil war, was an employee of S.N. Black, and married an Adams
    County lady at the close of the strife. He was married at the home of
    Mr Black.
WATTS, Twila   Sep 20, 1900
    See Phelps, Bert
WAYMAN, Miss Elizabeth V.   Jul 11, 1901
    See Seaton, Charles Drake
WEBSTER, Ernest   Augusta   Jan 3, 1901
    Ernest Webster and Miss Emma Simon were married Christmas Day at the home
    of officiating minister, Rev J. Stahl. Bride is daughter of Elmore Simon
    and wife. Groom is in the employ of F.M. King department store. Will live
    with his mother.
WEBSTER, Ernest   Augusta   Jan 3, 1901
    Ernest Webster and Miss Emma Simon were married Christmas Day at the resi-
    dence of the officiating minister, Rev J. Stahl.
WEBSTER, Wm   Dec 26, 1901
    See Hester, Wm
WEERT, Eilert Jr.   Local   Feb 15, 1902
    This eve at 7 o'clock at Prairie Church, Eilert Weerts, Jr and Miss Tina
    Flesner will be married by Rev Oetting. Edward Flesner will be groomsman
    and Miss Anna Weerts bridesmaid. Wedding supper to be given at home of
    brides parents. Will live on the old Weerts home place.
WEERTS, Miss Hirska   February 1893   Feb 21, 1901
    See Flessner, Gerd H.
WEHRMAN, Rev Charles   Wedding Bells   Dec 29, 1898
    Married last Thursday, Rev Charles Wehrman, pastor of the ME Church, in this
    city and Miss Mary Whray, only daughter of Dr and Mrs T.R. Whray at 7 PM by
    Rev Beadles. Mrs Mary McNeal of Bowen was bridesmaid and Harry Marsh was
    best man. Bride has taught school here several years. Rev Wehrman is in
    his second year as pastor of this church. They left Friday AM for Missouri
    to visit relatives of Rev Wehrman.

WEHRMAN, Rev Chas.   To be married Tonight   Dec 22, 1898
    This evening at 7:30 Rev Chas Wehrman, pastor of the ME Church and Miss Ma
    Whray will be married at the ME Church.
WEITIES, Miss Ella   Dec 25, 1903
    See Costigan, James
WELCH, Miss Dollie   Apr 10, 1897
    See Fletcher, Fred
WESSELS, Miss Christa   Nov 15, 1900
    See Craig, Wesley
WEST, Miss Myra   Mar 2, 1899
    See Donley, Thomas
WEST, Tobe   Augusta   Jan 3, 1901
    Invitations were issued last week announcing the marriage of Tobe West, of
    this place and Miss Lizzie Robinson, of Plymouth which will be solemnized
    at noon today, Wednesday at the home of brides parents. Groom is son of
    E.B. West and wife and is a partner with his father, in the meat market.
    Bride is one of Plymouth's fairest daughters. Will live in the property
    of the groom in the southeast part of town.
WEYEN, Frank   5 Years Ago   Sep 25, 1897
    Frank Weyen and Tena Zimmerman were married.
WEYEN, Miss Hannah   Mar 27, 1897
    See Ehnen, Aime
WEYEN, John   5 Years Ago   Jan 22, 1898
    John Weyen and Miss Kate Harberts were married Wednesday.
WEYEN, John   January 1893   Jan 17, 1901
    January 21   John Weyen and Miss Katie Harberts were married the 18th by
    Rev Darrow.
WEYEN, Miss Tena   Apr 3, 1903
    See Osterman, Habo
WHEELER, Amanda   Apr 27, 1899
    See Wolfe, John
WHEELER, Helen   Jul 18, 1896
    See Lyons, Mr and Mrs Louis
WHEELER, Joel E.   Local   Feb 10, 1905
    Joel E. Wheeler and Miss Mary McGartland, both of Camp Point were married
    at Quincy Wednesday by Rev Parker Shields.
WHITE, Daniel M.   Aug 9, 1900
    Daniel M. White, age 66, of Buckhorn, stated he needed a housemate. Last
    Friday he was lonely so he went to see Mrs Johanna Quinn, age 60, who also
    felt neglected. Result was they secured a license and went to Police
    Magistrate Wallace and were married.   "Democrat Message"
WHITE, Ed   Chatten   Mar 27, 1902
    Ed White and family attended the wedding of a relative Thursday at Elm Gro
WHITE, Miss Rebecca   Feb 8, 1896
    See Davis, Robert
WHITFORD, William J.   Apr 11, 1896
    See Sawtelle, Miss Jennie J.
WHITLAND, Miss Emma   Mar 21, 1901
    See Bienhoff, Henry
WHITTEN, Miss Florella   Jun 24, 1898
    See Newcomb, Jas. C.
WHRAY, Lewis E.   Jun 27, 1901
    See Chapman, Miss Cleora
WHRAY, Miss Mary   Dec 22, 1898
    See Wehrman, Rev Chas.

WILBURN, Miss Callie   Feb 28, 1901
   See Huff, George
WILHITE, Miss Cora   Nov 7, 1901
   See Siegal, John
WILKES, Fred   Bowen   Apr 5, 1896
   Fred Wilkes and Miss Electa Murtle were married last Saturday in Carthage.
WILLARD, Miss Ella   Fairview   Jul 17, 1902
   Word has been received from Miss Ella Willard, who went to Washington
   several months ago, that she married on July 3rd to Mr Lawrence King.
   They were married at the ME Church in Ritzville by Rev Fertig. Mr Philip
   Watkins and family were present at the wedding.
WILLARD, Hurley F.   Houston   Sep 14, 1899
   Hurley F. Willard and Miss Ada Jacobs were married at the home of T.M.
   Dillon in Camp Point last Thursday AM before going to the fair.
WILLARD, Miss Nellie   Houston   Mar 15, 1900
   Ralph Robertson and Miss Nellie Willard were quietly married at Bowen last
   Wednesday eve.
WILLET, Mr   Jan 28, 1898
   See Lierle, Miss Bessie
WILLIAMS, Charles and Laura   Round About US   Feb 22, 1896
   Charles Williams and Louisa Williams of Colchester were married at Macomb
   a short time ago. The couple were cousins and in consequence their mar-
   riage in this state was illegal, but did not know this until after the
   supposed union. They then proceeded to Burlington, Iowa and were remar-
   ried, the laws of that state permitting the marriage of cousins. "Ex"
WILLIAMS, George   Pea Ridge   Nov 16, 1895
   George Williams from near Mounds and Miss Cora Blansett of Pea Ridge were
   married at the home of the brides parents Thursday eve of last week.
WILLIAMS, Wilbur L.   Girl and The Man   Dec 2, 1897
   Wilbur L. Williams, whoe wife's suit for divorce was tried at present term
   of court, was arrested yesterday at his fathers home near Mt Sterling for
   abducting Mildred Carnahan from her home on York, Nebraska. Williams is in
   jail and Miss Carnahan wanted to be locked up with her lover. She is
   said to be only 16, thought she looks older. Williams wife lives in Quincy
   now. She was a Miss Hamilton and married Williams at her home in Clayton
   some seven years ago. He deserted her a couple years later and she came
   to Quincy with her father and Williams is an artist and drifted to York,
   Nebraska where he swindled the people out of several hundred dollars.
   "Whig", Tuesday.
WILLIAMS, Wilbur L.   Williams is Married   Jan 1, 1898
   Wilbur L. Williams whose wife applied for divorce from him in circuit court
   and who was arrested at the home of his parents near Mt Sterling on charge
   of abduction, has married the girl in case. Deputy sheriff came from York,
   Nebraska and nabbed him in Brown County. The girl he was charged with kid-
   napping was Mildred Carnahan who refused to appear against him as she said
   she went of her own will. Upon release he applied for and was granted a
   marriage license and Judge Wildman united in wedlock Williams and Mildred
   Carnahan. In marrying this Nebraska girl he has committed bigamy, for the
   decree of divorce has not yet been granted from his Quincy wife.
WILLIS, Miss Flora   Dec 18, 1897
   See Grigson, Fred R.
WILSON, Florence G.   Jan 3, 1901
   See Chambers, F.L. (Frank)
WINFIELD, Miss Fannie   Mar 29, 1900
   See Steele, Chas.

WINFIELD, George   LaPrairie   May 15, 1903
   Last Saturday at the home of Squire McCord occurred the wedding of George
   Winfield and Miss Florence Cox, both of this place.
WINFIELD, Sidney   LaPrairie   Mar 2, 1899
   Sidney Winfield, of this place, and Miss Anna Brady, of Carthage, were
   married Wednesday.
WINFIELD, Sidney   LaPrairie   Mar 9, 1899
   Sidney Winfield was married last Wednesday to Miss Anna Brady, of Carthage
   will live on Will Sickles farm.
WINSTON, James M.   Local   Jun 26, 1902
   James M. Winston, the popular Wabash conductor, was recently wedded to Mrs
   Mattie McMurray, of Clayton.
WISEHART, Ernest   May 30, 1901
   See Garrett, Miss Grace and Jennie
WISHART, Mary   Aug 29, 1896
   See Taylor, Tom
WITT, Adelia A.   Local   Aug 8, 1901
   Clifford W. Vaugh and Adelia A. Witt were married recently at Fresno, Cali
   fornia. Miss Witt was born and grew to womanhood in Houston township.
   She taught school here and in California where she held high salaried
   positions. Samuel and William Witt, of Houston, are her brothers.
WITT, Samuel   Primrose   Mar 24, 1894
   Samuel Witt, of Big Neck, was united in marriage to Miss Thomas, of Lorain
   Sunday.
WITT, Samuel   Review   Jun 12, 1902
   March 24, 1894 Samuel Witt, of Big Neck, and Miss Thomas, of Loraine,
   were married.
WITT, William   Primrose   Oct 17, 1895
   William Witt, one of the firm of Witt Bros., the well known cattle buyers,
   was married Wednesday to Miss Cella Andrews, of Mendon. Will live at his
   home in Big Neck.
WOLFE, John   Oldest Illinoisan   Apr 27, 1899
   "Uncle John" Wolfe of Liberty was a visitor in town Monday and can justly
   claim to be oldest native Illinoisan born near Jonesboro, Union County
   Aug 6, 1811. Came to Adams County when 20 years old. Located on section
   18 in what is now Liberty township and lived there since. Ten years later
   he married Amanda Wheeler and on May 4 they expect to celebrate their 58
   wedding anniversary. They have 8 children, six living, four daughters,
   two sons. He is a robust man nearly 88 years old and frequently walks to
   Liberty a distance of 1½ miles, attends his garden and grapevines. Saturday he drove to Coatsburg (9 or 10 miles) and Monday drove to Camp Point
   (14 miles) and back again. He had never lived outside the borders of the
   state and has lived nearly 68 years on one farm.
WOLFF, Anton Conrad   Local   Dec 19, 1902
   Anton Conrad Wolff, of Tonkawa, Oklahoma, and Miss Viola Hughes, of Golden
   were married by Judge McCrory at Quincy Tuesday afternoon.
WOODS, Miss Cecil Dora   Nov 20, 1903
   See Deane, Alfred G.
WOODS, Miss Charlotte   Apr 1, 1904
   At the home of James M. Stevens near LaPrairie at 3 PM Wednesday occurred
   the wedding of Herman C. Newnham and Miss Charlotte Woods. Will live at
   the home of H.C. Newnham near Augusta.
WOODS, George M.   Bowen   Mar 7, 1896
   George M. Woods and Miss Martha Morris were married at Antioch Church last
   Sunday eve by Esquire Charles Rockenfield. Reception at grooms fathers
   Zachariah Woods on the day following.

WOODWORTH, Stephen   Local   Nov 27, 1902
    Stephen Woodworth, of Clayton, and Anna Lydick of Shelbina, Missouri were
    married this week.
WORMAN, Miss Edna   Bethel Items   Aug 18, 1898
    Mr James Robbins of LaPrairie and Miss Edna Worman of Augsta were married
    by Rev Mathias last Tuesday eve.
WORMAN, Miss Lou   LaPrairie   Aug 3, 1899
    C.F. Schwanke and Miss Lou Worman, of Augusta, were married Thursday at
    7 AM and took the Fast Mail for their future home in Rockford, Illinois.
    Chas. is one of our best young men and has a good position on the C.B. & Q.
WORMAN, Miss Nellie   LaPrairie   Aug 21, 1903
    Marriage of Rev French and Miss Nellie Worman occurred at Washington Church
    on Thursday eve of last week.
WRIGHT, Walter   8 Years Ago   Sep 19, 1901
    July 22, 1893 Walter Wright and Miss Eva Ward of Pine Grove, were married.
WYSONG, Hebert   York Neck   Sep 23, 1904
    Mr Hebert Wysong, of Stillwell, and Miss Zephy Turner, of Woodville, were
    married in Quincy September 14th. Spent their honeymoon at the St Louis
    Fair.
WYSONG, Lee   Local   Jun 7, 1900
    Marriage license issued last week to Lee Wysong and Miss Eva Pressly, of
    Pine Grove neighborhood.
YACKLE, Edd   Pea Ridge   Aug 23, 1900
    Next Thursday occurs the wedding of Mr Edd Yackle and Miss Grace Upchurch.
YAGER, Silas E.   Nov 27, 1897
    See Mott, Miss Flora
YELDELL, Ernest   Clayton   Nov 3, 1898
    Marriage of Mr Ernest Yeldell and Miss Anna Moore was at the parsonage of
    the Congregational Church in Quincy by Dr Dana at 3 PM Wednesday. Mr
    Thomas Moore, father of the bride and Miss Tracy Bolinger were present.
    They will live with Mr and Mrs J.H. Yeldell on the farm.
YOUNG, Miss Abbey   Dec 20, 1900
    See Huey, Walter
YOUNG, Bertha   Apr 29, 1898
    See Hartly, Herbet
YOUNG, Miss Cora   Jan 3, 1901
    See Mickle, James
YOUNG, David   Jan 25, 1896
    See Hatcher, Mrs Helen
YOUNG, John W.   Oct 10, 1901
    See Owen, Miss Effie
YOUNGLOVE, James W.   Happy Event   May 27, 1904
    James W. Younglove of Cloud Cliff, Oklahoma and Miss Dora E. Clark, of this
    village were married at 10:30 at the parsonage of the Vermont St. Baptist
    Church in Quincy by Rev Harvey. Groom has been working as a telegraph
    lineman in Oklahoma and bride has been conducting a millinery store in this
    village, and they will make their home here.
ZIMMERMAN, Miss Angie   Feb 19, 1904
    See Busboom, Ollie
ZIMMERMAN, Tena   Sep 25, 1897
    See Weyen, Frank

Supplemental Information

JAMS, John and wife   Local   Jan 1, 1898
    John Adams and wife of Shelbina, Missouri are here visiting Mr and Mrs
    Will Downing and other friends. Mrs Adams was, until a few weeks ago
    known as, Miss Nellie Kern.
AMRINE, Bertha   Local   Jun 13, 1896
    Mounds, Illinois   Sunday eve Bertha and Jennie, daughters of Mr and Mrs
    John Amrine attended Sunday school. While exercises were going on Miss
    Bertha Amrine and Charles Lucas went off to Mt Sterling and were married
    at the home of Elmer Nokes.
BALLARD, Chas.   Review   Feb 6, 1902
    December 2, 1893 Married, Chas. Ballard and Miss Mary Berrian.
BIENHOFF, Audrey and Harm   Aug 28, 1902
    Public notice State of Illinois Circuit Court Adams County Illinois October
    term AD1902 #1440 Audrey Bienhoff, complaintant
                            vs   divorce
                    Harm Bienhoff, defendant
    said defendant having left the state of Illinois in August 1900 and his
    place of residence is unknown.   (dated Quincy August 20, 1902)
                        Hiram R. Wheat, clerk
BLEDSOE, Willis   The State   Jul 20, 1899
    Willis Bledsoe, a Warsaw boy, who only three weeks ago married Miss Jennie
    Hopkins, of the above city, was arrested for burglary in Denver, Colorado
    several days ago.   "Nauvoo Independent"
BUSS, Grace   8 Years Ago   Jul 4, 1901
    See Cassens, Wm
CLARK, Charles   Local   Nov 10, 1905
    Charles Clark and Miss Dora Kindhart surprised their friends Monday by going
    to Mt Sterling and returning Mr and Mrs Clark.
GORDON, Samuel   Local   Mar 27, 1903
    Samuel Gordon, of Ambrose and Miss Hila Hackney, of Elm Grove, were married
    in Quincy Wednesday.
HECOX, Oscar   Fowler   Apr 8, 1898
    Married last Thursday eve at LaPrairie, Oscar Hecox and Miss Jomattie King.
HOLECAMP, Francis   Pea Ridge   Mar 21, 1901
    Married last week, Mr Francis Holecamp and Miss Ausmus, of Mound Station.
HOPKINS, Miss Jennie   Jul 20, 1899
    See Bledsoe, Willis
HYNES, Wakeman   Loraine Tragedy   May 1, 1897
    New Era announced that Wakeman Hynes and Lizzie Hudson, uncle and niece had
    eloped. Such a mistake as their dead bodies were found in a wooded pasture
    Saturday, having been lying there since Sunday and during the rains of last
    week. It was a case of murder and suicide. Hynes had deliberately and
    seemingly with girls consent, shot her and then ended his own life.
KERN, Miss Nellie   Jan 1, 1898
    See Adams, John and wife
KIPP, Edward   Local   Apr 17, 1902
    Edward Kipp, of Quincy, and Iris M. Dunlap, of Bowen were married last week.
    Both bride and groom have many friends in Golden who wish them well.
MCCORMICK, John T.   Local   Mar 11, 1904
    John T. McCormick and Miss Lulu Murrah, of Coatsburg, were married this week.
MCMURRAY, J. Logan   Local   May 6, 1904
    Marriage license issued Monday to J. Logan McMurray of Clayton, and Miss Inez
    G. States, of same village.

RHEA, Miss Effie   Local
     Married, Wednesday, February 26th at the home of Mrs P. Rhea, Mr.
     Rhea to J. Fred Boger.   "Camp Point Journal"
ROWE, Henry   York Neck   Jun 6, 189~
     Wedding in Brushy last week, Henry Rowe and Miss Polena Reshell.
SCHONE, Miss Lena   Local   Feb 15, 1900
     Last Thursday at the West Side Church Rank Leenerts, of Golden and Miss Lena
     Schone, of Chatton were married by Rev Alpers. Will start housekeeping
     at their new home north of LaPrairie.
SCHRIVER, Frank   Fowler   Apr 8, 1898
     Married at the home of the bride, Frank Schriver and Miss Mattie Meyers,
     last week.
SCHWARTZ, Dr C.W.   Married   Jul 21, 1898
     Last eve at 6, at Topeka, Kansas, occured the marriage of two former Golden
     people, Dr C.W. Schwartz, of Camp Point and Miss Josie Strickler, of Topeka.
SLOAN, William   Review   Jun 12, 1902
     March 3, 1894   William Sloan and Miss Emma Wartick were married.
TENHAEFF, Fred   Historical   Apr 25, 1901
     April 22, 1893   Fred Tenhaeff and Miss Stella McCord were married.
VERTREES, Ray   Local   Feb 10, 1905
     Marriage licenses were issued at Quincy Monday to Ray Vertrees of Cleveland.
     Oklahoma and Miss Josie Harrah, of Bushnell. Mr Vertrees is a former reside
     of LaPrairie and is a nephew of Charles N. Vertrees.
WISHART, Charlie   Camp Point   Sep 8, 1899
     Since last week, the wedding of Charlie Wishart and Miss Bertha Baird took
     place at the home of the bride, by Rev Dillon.

Heritage Books by
Mrs. Joseph J. Beals, Sr. and Mrs. Sandra Kirchner:

Births and Related Items Abstracted from The Camp Point Journal
of Camp Point, Adams County, Illinois, 1873–1903

Deaths Abstracted from The Camp Point Journal, *1873–1882,*
Camp Point, Adams County, Illinois

Deaths Abstracted from The Camp Point Journal, *1883–1892,*
Camp Point, Adams County, Illinois

Deaths Abstracted from The Camp Point Journal, *1893–1903,*
Camp Point, Adams County, Illinois

Marriages (1895–1905) and Deaths (1895–1900) and Related Items Abstracted
from the Golden New Era *of Golden, Adams County, Illinois*

Marriages and Related Items Abstracted from The Clayton Enterprise
Newspaper of Clayton, Adams County, Illinois, 1879–1900

Marriages and Related Items Abstracted from the Mendon Dispatch
of Mendon, Adams County, Illinois, 1877–1905

Obituaries and Death Related Items Abstracted from Clayton Enterprise
Newspaper of Clayton, Adams County Illinois, 1879–1900, Volume 1

Obituaries and Death Related Items Abstracted from the Hendon Dispatch
of Mendon, Adams County, Illinois, 1877–1905

CD: Births and Deaths Abstracted from The Camp Point Journal,
Camp Point, Adams County, Illinois, 1873–1903

CD: Marriages and Related Items Abstracts from the Golden New Era
Newspaper of Golden, Adam County, Illinois, 1895–1905

CD: Marriages and Related Items Abstracts from the Mendon Dispatch
of Mendon, Adams County, Illinois, 1877–1905

CD: Obituaries and Death Related Items Abstracts from the Golden New Era
Newspaper of Golden, Adam County, Illinois, 1895–1900

CD: Obituaries and Death Related Items Abstracts from the Mendon Dispatch
of Mendon, Adams County, Illinois, 1877–1905